Revered Moments

Altamese Moore

Copyright © 2013 Altamese Moore
All rights reserved.

ISBN: 0615780164
ISBN-13: 9780615780160
Library of Congress Control Number: 2013904224
Aloe Expressions, Glendale, Wisconsin

I thank God for His divine guidance, and I thank all of my family for their unwavering support.

PART 1
Cruising With God

Inspiration	2
Along the Gulf	3
Reflections	4
What is it That You Seek?	6
Early Intervention	6
Early Education	7
Always a Treat	8
Sweet Potatoes	9
A Family Name Says a Lot	9
Planting a Seed	10
Dream and Renew	11
Valuable	12
Declutter to Restore	12
The Miracle Trip	13
Travel	15
In His Hands	15
His Creation	16
A Tell Tale Interview	17
Finding Hope	18
God's Timing	18
Sometimes I Think	19
Crash	20
January 2nd	21
Kindness Rules!	21
Mystery	22
Here	22

An Agonizing Thought	23
You Should be Responsible for Something	23
Plant Your Seed	24

PART 2
God Prepares the Way

Advantage	28
An Observation	28
The One	29
Our Own Oasis	29
Forge Ahead	31
Neighbor	32
God Leads the Way	32
Free to Soar	33
Victory	34
Wow!	34
Artificial Barriers	35
My Father's Eyes	35
Myths	36
Car Troubles	37
Sunny	38
The Simplest of Things	38
How Does Your Garden Grow?	39
Scale	40
A State of Flux	40
My Voice	42
Imperfection	42
Coupons	42
Where's Your Joy?	43
Not My Friend	44
Pits	45
Cleaning	46
Arrogance	46
Follow Your Path	47

PART 3
A Place in God's Hammock

An Angel From Above	50
Suddenly	51
Motivation	51
Hyper Spirituality	52
Mary Williams	53
Bring It to the Light	53
In the Lord	54
Popsicle	55
Experience	55
Composure	56
Weariness	56
Once an Enemy, Now My Friend	57
Arm & Hammer Baking Powder	58
Judy	59
Confirmation	59
An Airport Vendor	60
Shirley	60
The Lure of Fame and Riches	61

PART 4
The Blackboard is Everywhere

Learning Without Walls	64
Not Far Away	64
A Surrounding View	65
Solace	66
Off to College	67
Lessons Learned From Animals	68
The Rabbit and the Blackbird	69
Unusual Events Require Unusual Actions	70
He's Real	71
Colors	72
A Change in Seasons	72
A Church Appearance	73

Use What You Have	74
A Good Samaritan	75

PART 5
Absorbed in the Light

A Pick From Nature	78
Designer Threads	78
Ducks?	79
For Me	79
Pure Light	79
Composure	81
Faith	81
Always There	82

PART 6
A God-like State of Mind

Just Stop It!	84
What would Jesus Say?	84
You Never Know Unless You Try	84
Infinite is He	86
Bliss	86
Still in Control	86
Hands Down	87
Himalaya	88

PART 7
The Spirit of Christmas

Anticipation	90
The Selfishness in Humanity	90
Christmases of Old	91
Christmas Tree	92
A Brown Paper Bag	93
Glitter	93
The Biggest Gift Ever	94
Never Forget	94
Final Thoughts	95

Introduction

We have taken the time to chart our trip, and we have packed our boats with all of the essentials that are needed to help us survive the long voyage; so we go out to sea. As we cruise across the waves and gaze upon the stars at night, our hopes and dreams are kept alive, because we get closer to our destination with the passing of each day.
But as we continue to sail, our sunny skies begin to turn into overcast skies, and without any warning, our overcast skies turn into sunny skies, leaving us confused and not knowing what to expect from day to day. And it is on these days, when we are pushed away from the course we originally set that, we find ourselves visiting places that we never imagined. Some of us have been blown off course time after time. Although this is unexpected and can be frustrating at times, it fits in perfectly with God's plans.
I, too, had traveling plans, a strategy, and a timeline for navigating through this world. However, these plans have changed so many times throughout the years as I have rowed through many uncharted waters. I believe God has already set a course for us before we enter this world, and through prayer, we must continuously ask Him to guide us to the right path.

After my work as a teacher and administrator came to an end, I needed to chart a new course for my life. In doing so, I was constantly having to battle with the fear of not knowing where I would go. The waves kept getting bigger with the passing of each day. So I continued to pray, asking God to show me His will for my life. I know that God is always with us, and He does answer prayers. Two such times when God revealed His glory to me will always remain etched in my mind. On both occasions, God sent a visible angelic being to open doors that I could not. I describe each of these stories in later sections of this book.

God continues to give me guidance through what I have termed "knocks." They come in the form of words that are spoken, written, or thought by me and simultaneously spoken by someone from the radio or television. These knocks have occurred at various times. Receiving knocks is like finding rocks that mark the path to a specific destination. I do believe that God is guiding me through these knocks, because I have to be where I am at that given moment in time in order to hear them.

Throughout my cloudy days, God has created opportunities that I could never imagine. When I had almost given up on realizing my goal of finding enjoyable and purposeful employment, He delivered. If He did this for me, He can do it for you too. I encourage you to tune in to God and ask for His help should you find yourself in need of chartering a new course for your life. Pay attention to those moments that happen time after time that one could easily dismiss as just happenstance.

The reason I wrote this book is because I eyewitnessed two inexplicable divine experiences. We are not alone. This book is meant to inspire and encourage you to seek your connection to God and to ask Him to show you what His will is for your life as you journey through this world. Throughout the book, I share with you my understanding of God and the world through my personal stories and experiences with divine happenings, quotes, poems, and philosophical thoughts as I travel toward spiritual growth and my divine purpose in life. God's wonders are all around us and can be seen in nature and through the actions of others. There are sections in the book where I encourage you to write your comments or thoughts after reading the ones I have provided. At the back of the book are pages where you can write down your own thoughts and knocks. Use this book as a catalyst to stimulate further discussions among family, friends, and acquaintances.

My prayer for all is that we get to live a life inspired by God—a life of purpose, love, and joy—and that when we fall, and we will, our faces are looking toward the heavens. Amen!

Part 1
Cruising with God

Inspiration

It happened again mid-September. Normally, the Bible that I have on my nightstand stays open. There is something about keeping the Bible open so that God's words can permeate the air. But on this particular morning, the Bible was closed. My husband had taken it downstairs to read and returned it to the nightstand during the night, closed. So the next morning, I randomly opened it without looking at the location.

Later that afternoon, I got the mail from our mailbox and began to shuffle my way through the letters. Surprisingly, one of the letters came from a spiritual leader that I had contacted a few months earlier. As I read the letter, the book of Job was referenced as he continued to talk about Job's faithfulness to God and his ultimate triumph over evil. After a brief period of time, I went upstairs. While there, I went over to the Bible, and intending to turn to the book of Job, I found that the Bible was already opened to Job. I ask you, was my random opening of the Bible to the book of Job a coincidence or much more?

My belief is that God sends us messages all the time. If we ask God to direct our paths and believe that He will, miraculous things will manifest in our lives. Each happening will have perfect timing and leave you knowing that God is in charge; He is guiding you as He has guided many people during biblical times. These manifestations are purposeful and not accidental.

Because God knew us before we knew ourselves, He personalizes our messages. Have you ever spoken to a stranger, and through your conversation, a thought you had been contemplating was affirmed by something they said? Maybe you heard a lot of depressing words and saw painful actions coming from people, who represent the worst in humanity, and it saddened your soul, but later on that day, a stranger displayed an act of kindness—a smile, kind word, or a deed such as opening a door for you, and your soul rejoiced. Occurrences like these reaffirm my belief that good will always triumph over evil.

Today I am pushing away busy work, and I am focusing on writing this book. I have always enjoyed writing but lacked the long-term discipline that writing requires. Yesterday one of the leaders of the church said during service that a journey begins with the first step. Motivated by his inspiring words, I started my journey by writing the first of many words, and I invite you to come along with me. As Joshua 1:9 says, "For the Lord thy God is with thee whithersoever thou goest."

Along the Gulf

From dusk until dawn, He watches all the time.

We had only been in this new town for a few hours before we needed to drive to our next destination. Leaving our belongings at the hotel, we carefully followed our computer-generated directions through the city. As we traveled down the long street, we could see a huge wooden structure. It resembled a straw hut that you would see next to a beach. A few yards from it was the vast waters of the Gulf of Mexico. My husband, children, and I were there to attend the rehearsal dinner in honor of a friend who was getting married that weekend.

The inside of the building was as intriguing as the outside. One side of the building had no walls, only wooden picnic tables with matching benches. In the middle of the floor was an area for dancing. There were jugglers, volleyball games, and upbeat dance music played by a disc jockey in the outside area. Meanwhile, beads of sweat continued to roll down our faces and along our spines as we greeted new arrivals and tried to relax after our long journey to Gulf Port, Alabama. An hour later, John arrived and sat at our table.

In the crowded building, as guest and patrons moved in all directions, John, a long-time friend, began to tell us about his experience driving from the nearest airport to the rehearsal dinner. He said that he had leased a convertible but didn't have enough time to figure out how to put the top down, since he worried about getting to the rehearsal dinner on time.

John's story was funny and made our situation much more comfortable. In a lighthearted voice, he continued his story by telling us that as he headed down the highway, there were cars moving slowly in both lanes. This made it impossible for him to pass in either lane, causing him to eagerly wait for an opportunity to pass the slower traffic. John said that all he could think about was getting to the rehearsal dinner on time. So when the opportunity came, he quickly sped around the cars. As he glanced at the slower drivers, he could see the expressions on their faces, and they seemed to be asking the question, "Where are you going?" Now, I am asking you the same question, "Where are you going?"

Reflections

Allow the Lord to reign deep in your heart now and forever-more, and you will always have a soft place to dwell.

Life is an experiment orchestrated by God: the final grade is Pass or Fail. Which category do you think you fall under? There is no in between. At the end of the experiment, God will be the only judge and will separate the good from the bad.

We have to look at our own lives. How are you doing? Do you believe that there is a God? If so, do you live a life that coincides with the teachings of God? Do we love our neighbors because they are human beings, made by God and allowed to exist in this world? Are you able to stand behind God's truths and deny evil whatever form it comes in? Do you use God's truths as a platform to guide and help you make all decisions?

God's truth guides my life and strengthens me when I am weak. When decisions have to be made and sadness comes, or when happiness comes, I only need to bow my head, pray, and give thanks. God is always there, and it is with this knowledge that I am sharing some of my personal experiences with you.

As I look around, I see many, many people engaging in activities that are in opposition to God's teachings. For example, people who hate others because they belong to a different racial, economic, or ethnic group. Yet, these same people profess to be Christians while blatantly ignoring that God says that we are to love our neighbors. God will take our lives to where he wants them to go—if we allow him to. This movement reminds me of a game that I use to play as a child called "connect the dots." The goal of the game was to keep connecting dots and looking for opportunities to be the player to connect the last two dots, forming a square, thus claiming that square as your own (putting the initial of your first name in it.) The player with the most squares win. Through a series of calculated moves, God takes us from one point to the next, and ultimately, we end in a comfortable and peaceful place.

How often do we spend time with ourselves? I think so many people are afraid to spend time alone because they come to know that they have nothing in common with themselves. As long as there are other people around us day and night, or we have somewhere to be or go, we do not have to confront our true selves. We do not have to think about some of the answers to complex questions such as what we really like or dislike, or how we can honor God's teachings while existing in this world.

There was a period in my life when I did not want to think about the time when my children would be away at college and my husband away at work; I would then be alone. I thought that having a job would fill some of the extra time and would make the transition to empty-nester easier. Guess what? I was still unemployed when the economy went into a recession, and my children went away from home—a long way off: New York. I felt the burden of trying to figure out how to manage my time during this transition, with or without a job.

Now, I had to restructure my time while I familiarized myself with the true but new me. This period in my life was challenging and difficult, but not welcoming change was selfish. When I resisted the idea that change had come, my inner conflicts and battles grew stronger. As I began to accept change and acknowledge that this is a constant allowed by God, I was better able to tap into my creative side and reinvent my life. I accepted this as a part of God's plan for my life.

So, I invite and encourage anyone who feels that their life is in need of a recharge or restructuring to steal some alone time. During this process, you may find yourself reconnecting with some of the skills and talents that you have long abandoned and using them to bring enjoyment to new activities. There are so many God-given skills and talents that are waiting to be discovered. Take some time to better yourself.

Finding time alone can be difficult because some of us are so caught up in our problems and other people's problems, and are so busy trying to survive the day that we often overlook the signs God sends to us. To get our attention, He does deeds that are so out of the ordinary that they get our immediate attention. Each one is uniquely designed with lessons that, if learned, will bring us closer to His will and purpose for our lives.

Through inward reflection, I know God is telling me that I am where I should be as He guides me on the path that He wants me to take. No longer do I have to wonder if I should be doing something else or be somewhere else. I encourage you to slow down long enough so that you can see and hear what God is telling you.

What Is It that You Seek?

A pond with ducks flanked by cattails,
The running river with blueberry bushes to the side,
That sea that flows into the ocean,
What is it that you seek?

A hill for planting seeds of choice,
The mound from which to play
Or the mountain that overlooks the valley
What is it that you seek?

Land—just a spot to plant your feet,
A plot of it to build,
Acres and acres for the view,
What is it that you seek?

Early Intervention

*Clear the vision around so you will have
clearer vision inside.*

One of the earliest memories I have of divine intervention and protection happened when I was around six or seven years of age. It took place early on a Saturday morning, and it was becoming hotter with each passing hour in the small town of Holly Hill, South Carolina. This was a perfect day to build a wagon.

I remember roaming around my mother's and grandparents' yards to find things to build a wagon. Kneeling on the ground next to my mother's back porch steps, I tried to figure out where I could find a fourth wheel to complete my wagon. Just then, I saw an amazing red tire, just the top half, draped over and through some weeds. It was among a pile of rusty cans and other discarded odds and ends. As I started to walk toward the pile, a clear and audible voice in my head directed me to throw something toward the red wheel. I did, and it moved.

Running as fast as I could up the many steps, which were made of stacked cement blocks that led into my grandparents' house, I told my grandfather what happened. My grandfather grabbed his gun and ran to the site. He fired his gun, but the snake quickly slithered away. It was a big red water moccasin. I neither finished building my wagon nor spent much time in the yard for the rest of the day. Over the years, I have kept this memory close to my heart, and I am forever reminded of God's grace and mercy. He is always watching over us and protects us when we face danger or when our lives are about to make a transition to another level.

Early Education

The Lord is growing me.

I was born in the country in a little area called Boyer. It is located about two miles from the town of Holly Hill, South Carolina, which is about forty-five miles west of Charleston, South Carolina. From an early age, education has always been an important part of my life. By the time I went to first grade, my grandmother had taught me how to write my name, count, recite, and write the alphabet. My grandfather helped me with my reading assignments every day after spending eight-plus hours at work. I remember taking pieces of chalk from sheetrock and using it to write on the walls of the old barn that stood between my grandparents' and my mother's houses. Years later, as an adult, I would revisit the old barn on many occasions to stare at my early writings as a child.

Above all, I am grateful for God, the Master Teacher, who gave me loving and strong parents. They helped me learn valuable lessons, but more importantly they introduced me, at an early age, to an omnipotent God who is able to walk, comfort, and guide me through any problem that may arise in this world.

Always a Treat

Touching someone mimics the action of a raindrop falling in a puddle.

Before I was old enough to attend school, my grandmother would carry me with her to take my grandfather to work early in the morning and to pick him up from work in the evening. When the sawmill's five o' clock whistle blew, I knew my grandfather would soon be coming down the path. I'd recognize him instantly, since he stood over six feet tall. There he walked among the other men, carrying a metal lunchbox, as they made their way down the rocky path. I would jump out of the car and run to meet him. Occasionally, my grandfather allowed me to visit him at his place of work. I can still remember the smell of hot pine as steam constantly radiated from the logs as they passed along the outer edge of the room where my grandfather worked. I watched him as he masterfully used a machine to move the newly arrived logs from one place on the yard to another.

Weekends were special at my grandparents' house. Every Friday after my grandfather got off from work, we would buy groceries. Near the checkout counter was a machine that roasted peanuts. The peanuts were placed in snack-size brown bags with rolled down rims and twisted corners. The aroma from the roasted peanuts was the first scent you smelled as you walked into the store. My grandfather would sometimes grab a bag or two bags of roasted peanuts from the shelf. At other times, he would buy raw peanuts and roast them at home. When we were blessed with an abundance of fresh peanuts grown in our garden, my grandparents would dry some and store them for the fall, and the others were boiled as an early fall treat.

Frequently, on Saturdays, my grandparents would bake sweet potatoes on top of a black potbelly stove that was also used to heat the house. The smell from the sweet potatoes baking scented the whole house. Not only did the old potbelly stove provide warmth to the body but it also warmed the heart.

Sweet Potatoes

A black potbelly stove
Extended a foot from the wall
Filled with logs and splinters
That crackles throughout the house
Warms the soul during fall and winter.

Sweet potatoes roasting on top
Emit a scent that transcends others
Spicy, alluring, exotic it travels
Warming the heart and opening the mind,
Savoring this moment in time.

The room fills as each draws near
Around the old potbelly stove
Watching and waiting with anticipation
To feast when the potatoes are finally done.

A Family Name Says a Lot

Other people are counting on you, so count on yourself—believe!

When I was growing up, people who were meeting you for the first time would ask, "Who are your people?" Having a good family name opened up many opportunities, because it represented a person coming from a family with good character and moral standing in the community. Whenever I had to use my family's name, it was greeted with a smile and followed by positive comments.

Are people interested anymore in maintaining a good name? In today's society, some people seem to be in constant motion and not residing in a place long enough to care to develop positive relationships in the community. Should we adopt an attitude that no matter where or how long we reside in an area, treating people with decency and respect is the right thing to do? It appears that some people deliberately engage in activities that would be considered morally questionable and offensive by the larger society, because they can use the lack of community ties as an excuse to clear their conscience of wrongdoing.

All of the traits that help create a good name are traits found in God's teachings: love, truth, respect, faith, and integrity. (I'm sure that you could continue to add to this list.) The right thing should be done in the dark and in the light. For those of us who believe that having a good name is still important, let's continue to use this value as a standard while interacting with others on a daily basis. Furthermore, let us plant a seed, one that grows valuable fruit and yields its goodness in our children. Giving our children a good family name to grow into is a wonderful gift that renews itself from one generation to the next.

Planting a Seed

With anticipation we wait
As the soil is being churned,
The field at the back of the house
Where once stood weeds and many stubby trees,
Reveals barren and huge crumpled rows
Of rich darkened soil from which plants will grow.

My grandparents, mother, siblings, and I
Use our tools – hoes and rakes
To chop through the clumps and smooth the bumps,
Leaving in front of us as we go
A picture of beauty with an inviting canvas,
Just waiting for the seeds we plan to sow.

> Returning to our point of origin,
> We scoop out pockets to make a place,
> Counting our seeds, putting them in and saying
> 'Good night'
> To corn, melons, peas and beans,
> Okra, tomatoes, cucumbers, greens,
> Peppers, sweet potatoes and peanuts,
> All to yield when the time is right.

Dream and Renew

The only person that can see your dream in to reality is you.

    I am sitting in my office (kitchen) at the desk (kitchen table), and it dawns on me: "I don't dream anymore." When I was younger, especially in my twenties, I would imagine the possibilities and set positive goals. But as I took on more responsibilities in my life, dreaming was pushed so far back that it disappeared. It was not until my circumstances changed and the pressures downsized that I had moments of quiet time to rekindle my faint dreams. I could not do this under my own strength. I needed the strength that could only come from the Creator. And through prayer, God allowed me to start dreaming again. Recapturing my dreams was worth the effort.

    When we are able to dream, we have hope, which leads to faith and stirs us to action. As a result, we are better able to show our children and other people how to start or how to reclaim their dreams. There will be many obstacles to test your commitment, perseverance, and strength when trying to realize a dream; and knowing this helps to cope with setbacks. But remember that you are valuable, your children are valuable, and people are valuable.

    So when the heavy rains come and you can barely see, grab your umbrella and brace yourself against the harsh winds. Nourish your dreams and continue to grow. Stand in a position grounded in divine strength.

Valuable

The bell rings and she runs to the bus,
Zigzagging through and around the city
It slows and comes to an abrupt halt,
Knock on the door and nobody comes,
Need to get in and search for a key,
How valuable is she—How valuable is she?

Her little brother follows in her steps
As they look high and low around and about,
This had happened before—too many times to count,
Knock on the door and nobody comes,
Mom is somewhere roaming free,
How valuable is he—How valuable is he?

They push through a window to let themselves in,
Dogs barking in the alley, and unknown faces passing,
Reaching back and putting things as they were
Nobody's home—neither mom nor dad,
Quite unusual, disturbing some would say,
How valuable are they—How valuable are they?

Declutter to Restore

Stop living a life of accumulation.

    A couple of storms passed through during the night and continued into the morning with loud thunder and lightning, racing wind, and rain. I wished I could have slept a little longer, but my mind began to fill with empty thoughts; I began to feel restless, because there was not anything in particular that I needed to do on this day. The dampness from the outside made the house feel cold, and somehow my mind associated this feeling with the idea that I needed to do some housecleaning and restore a sense of warmth. Weird? For the rest of the day, I began to declutter the house by throwing away old, stored newspapers and magazines. It is amazing how a small action can yield big results. As clarity was restored, I was able to dismiss thoughts with no rational basis, setting a better mood for the day.

To get closer to God, we have to get rid of anything we have accumulated that stands between us and God. When this is done, our minds are clearer, and we are more receptive to the hearing of and the application of God's words to our lives. We will always feel warm, sharing this warmth with others as we travel throughout the world.

Now, take inventory of your physical and mental clutter and dump it into your trash bin.

The Miracle Trip

*Up and down the hills we go, not knowing what we'll find.
But whatever it is, I do know it's what God has in mind.*

We were in the car and driving toward Minot, North Dakota. My brother had just retired from the Air Force after committing over twenty years of service. He had been deployed at least three times to Iraq. I remember getting the last phone call just before he was about to be sent on a mission. How do you handle such a call? Throughout our conversation, I felt nervous and did my best to fight back the tears. This was a trying time for all the family. Over the months, I continued to pray, read my Bible, talk to God, and keep a mental picture of God cloaking my brother underneath his mighty wings. So, this trip to Minot was very special.

We had a smooth ride all the way from Milwaukee to just outside of Minneapolis, exhaling as we passed by green open fields, nestled lakes, and familiar and unfamiliar sights. Meandering on the interstate, we could all see darkened skies and flashes of lightning in the distance. Any time we travel far away from home, we are constantly watching the needle on the gas gauge. This time, we could see that we needed to buy some gas, because we only had about a quarter of a tank left. The thunder continued to roll, and the flashes of light lit up the darkening skies. Yet, we cruised by the gas station because my husband felt that we had enough gas to make it to the next gas station. Well, we continued to look for other gas stations with worried eyes mile after mile.

It started to pour down rain; we had entered the path of a thunderstorm. The day had turned to night. We stared out of the windows, hoping to catch a glimpse of any station. Praying silently for God's help and guidance, I could see a car coming down the lane to the left of us. As it moved a little in front of us, I could not clearly see the driver or the passenger because of its tinted windows. It was a cream-colored Honda Accord. My first brand-new car was a Honda Accord, back in the late eighties. The back of the car now visible to me, I could see its license plate. It read, "Prayer Changes Things." A word of affirmation, I thought, and pointed it out to my husband and children.

I thought that the car would continue to zoom down the road, but it didn't. It stayed just ahead of us as if it was guiding us mile after mile. I felt a sense of peace and comfort. I continued to pray as we turned off of the interstate onto another highway while the Honda Accord continued down the interstate.

After riding a few miles on this new highway, it struck me that there were no homes and no stores of any kind. However, there were many electrical poles flanking the road. Another strange item: only trucks traveled the road. We were the only car on the highway, and we were in dire need of gas. So my husband decided to trail in the draft behind a semi-truck just in front of us. It just seemed like an eternity as we continued to drift down the highway.

Suddenly, the semi-truck reduced its speed, and so did we. We were entering the city limits of a small town. The stores along the streets were dark, but we could see a few people walking on the sidewalk. Praying and hoping that we would spot an open gas station, our prayers and hopes were realized when we saw one up ahead. We were happy that there was a gas station but disappointed because it was closed. Pulling into the lot and scanning the gas pump, we quickly came to the realization that this pump was available twenty-four hours a day and accessible with the use of a credit card. Relieved and full of thanks, we filled the tank. Somewhere between one and two o'clock, we arrived at my brother's house.

As the license plate says, "Prayer Changes Things." It does. Praying should be our first line of defense. Next, move forward with faith, purpose, and the unshakable strength that only comes from God to accomplish daily tasks and dreams.

Travel

Traveling refreshes my soul,
As day turns into night
Or night turns into day,
I'm somewhere—some place,
Interacting with unfamiliar sights.

Traveling refreshes my soul,
My thoughts realign into something I recognize,
Making sense of what I could not see before,
Restoring my will to take a different path
And using that to create a better life.

I travel because it helps me grow,
There's a big wide world I'm longing to know,
With so many miles and seas to cross,
Reconnecting to the source
That allows these possibilities:
God.

In His Hands

I cannot speculate, because I cannot see what the Lord has in store for me, but I do know that it is going to be great!

I slept late this morning, because I did some extensive landscaping on the front yard yesterday. I trimmed the evergreen trees surrounding the porch, and I also raked off the red lava rocks to lay some landscaping fabric to prevent the weeds from returning. After getting up, I opened the blinds to my bedroom window and saw a beautiful border surrounding the front entrance. This gave me a sense of accomplishment. Then I went downstairs to open the curtains covering the living room window and open the blinds in the kitchen.

I thought about my dream from last night, but my thoughts were interrupted when I saw something moving by my orange flowering rose bush. Without my eyeglasses, I couldn't tell what it was, so I grabbed them and ran back to the patio door. It was a robin—an overweight robin with a very noticeable protruding breast. I continued to watch as it flew and perched on top of an electrical wire, causing it to shake each time the robin moved.

My mind reflected on the passage found in Matthew 6:26: "Behold the fowls of the air: for they sow not, neither do they reap, nor gather into barns; yet your heavenly Father feedeth them. Are ye not much better than they?"

It is this knowing that I write:

His Creation

This is how we come
From Him that made us,
Curly hair, black skin,
Creative and unique,
A part of His plan,
Molded by His will and hands.

This is how we come
From Him that made us,
Straight hair, white skin,
Creative and unique,
A part of His plan,
Molded by His will and hands.

This is how we come
From Him that made us,
Straight hair, honey skin,
Creative and unique,
A part of His plan,
Molded by His will and hands.

This is how we come
From Him that made us,
Curly hair, straight hair,
Black, Brown, White and Honey Skin,
Green, Brown, Blue and Black Eyes,
An assortment of many—Humanity,
All creative and unique,
All a part of His plan,
Molded by His will and hands.

A Telltale Interview

Never quit your fight before reaching your full potential.

During my stint of long-term unemployment, I finally got an invitation for an interview. The part-time position involved helping students improve their literacy skills in reading and math. Although I wanted to find a full-time job, I remained hopeful about the possibility of getting a part-time job. On the day of the interview, I arrived early. One lady came out and introduced herself as the interviewer. She then searched for a room where the interview could be conducted. After searching for a few minutes, she informed me that the interview would be conducted in the open atrium. As I sat there gathering myself for the interview, I could see people passing around me and even taking a seat in a nearby area.

The interview got started, and I felt comfortable about my responses to her questions. Soon we were joined by another lady, who the interviewer introduced as a supervisor at one of the literacy sites; she also participated in the questioning session. Toward the end of the interview, the interviewer asked, "You are aware that this is a part-time job?" After hearing this, I knew that the chances of me getting this job was slim to none, with the latter being the case.

I went home feeling disappointed but vowing to continue my job search and remain hopeful. While moving through the various job sites on the Internet, I came across one that I thought was well suited for my talents and skills, so I began to fill out the online application. In the background, I was listening to my hand-cranked radio.

As I labored through the long application process, I finally came to the last part, which requested the names and addresses of references. I had already typed the information for two of my references and had just started on the third reference. My third reference's name is "Cynthia." With an open ear to the radio, the host of my favorite local talk radio station introduced his next guest as "Cynthia." I stopped typing and wondered in amazement. Was this another coincidence?

Finding Hope

I will deny self-doubt when I see her again
Or maybe him, they change so conveniently,
Aiming to block my vision of what could be
And keeping me in a constant state of uncertainty.

A conversation with him or her I'd rather not have,
There is so much potential within I want to release,
But this self-doubt, if allowed, agitates and diminishes
The goodness, creativity, causing all to cease.

Tired of playing this game especially within my life,
Dropped head, drooped shoulders and dragging feet,
I wrap my arms around a fleeting spark of hope
And hang on until I regain my strength.

God's Timing

Because the Lord is able, He enables me.

The steam from my cup of morning tea continues to rise as I sit at the kitchen table while twirling a pencil back and forth through my fingers, hoping to create a poem and write it to paper. I push for an idea, a word, a theme—nothing. My mind wanders back to when I was a student in elementary school. I remember writing some pretty good stories and poems; my drawings weren't bad either. Many of my favorite drawings were pictures of tall mountains covered with trees that surrounded small lakes. What scenes did you draw in school? I would draw these scenes when I zoned out from my teacher's lectures. These nature pictures made me feel warm and peaceful inside. But now creativity felt so far away.

After trying to come up with a good poem and having no luck for almost an hour, I get up from the kitchen table and walk away, feeling disappointed. As I go about my day, I pray and ask God to help me tap into my creative side so that I can write some good poems. I think about all the inspiration that surrounds me: the mighty oak trees in my backyard, bountiful flowering rose bushes, a lush vegetable garden, birds, squirrels, and an occasional deer. However, the words do not flow today.

The next morning I am sitting down at the kitchen table sipping tea and praying for a different outcome today. I begin to write and write and write. The words come as easily as the liquid flowing from my cup. I complete my first poem, a second, and then a third poem. This happening reminds me of one of my grandmother's favorite sayings: "He may not come when you want Him, but He's right on time." God has perfect timing, and this concept goes beyond our human understanding.

For the next couple of months, my cup runneth over. I always carry a pen and a notepad with me, because I never know when inspiration will hit. I compose poem after poem. Writing poems provides me with structure and purpose and helps me to better deal with a frustrating, challenging, and changing time in my life.

Sometimes I Think

I am reminded of the squirrel
That chips out a hole in the tree
To ready itself for what's sure to come,
Even though it's not here today,
Sometimes I think.

The geese that pluck through the grass
To find remnants of something to eat,
For tomorrow they travel elsewhere
Because they surely know what's to come,
Even though it's not here today,
Sometimes I think.

Leaves flutter through the air
Landing on the green and brown tweed carpet below,
They too know that this must be done
To protect their host from possible harm,
Even though it's safe for today,

Thrown away things that stay around,
Over and over, time after time
Without thought for today or tomorrow,
Will come back to remind us
In ways unimaginable,
Sometimes I think, and think and think.

Crash

    This is the first day of the new year, and the Christmas tree is still standing in front of our living room window. This is my attempt to hold on to all of the good feelings surrounding the holidays. I'm not the only one. As I drive through the neighborhood, I still see blazing lights emanating from Christmas trees, on outside trees, and on shrubs. In years past, my neighbors have kept their Christmas decorations up way past February. So in comparison, I'm feeling okay with having my Christmas tree standing in its familiar place.
    A year ago, I bought a puzzle book from Borders, a book store, because I enjoyed the challenge of trying to solve a puzzle on cold, snowy mornings. This book contains three hundred and fifty puzzles. I begin to flip through the book to find the one that I would try to solve, when I spot the right one. As I begin to write in each letter of the answer for one clue,

each letter into its own square, forming the word "crash," a woman's voice from a commercial on television says, "crash." This is perfect timing.

Is there any explanation other than divine intervention for such an occurrence? Well, you might be saying at this moment, "It's just a matter of chance." That's okay too, but stay with me as we continue to explore these knocks.

January 2nd

The second day in the new year
And once again I sit
Trying to figure out which path to take
To inspire, grow—moves to make.

Blessed, I can hear the birds singing
And I can now see the sun shining
But on the horizon, rainy ice is coming,
Today, I embrace, tomorrow may not be as kind.

Kindness Rules!

Quiet the thoughts in your head by engaging others in the outside world.

Last night, I had trouble falling asleep: I felt restless. So when I woke up this morning, I did not feel like going anywhere or doing anything. Eventually, I forced myself to make up the bed and wash dishes. Yesterday, I decided that I would go to the grocery store today. Without thinking too much about the dreadful trip, I got dressed and went on my way. The workers at the grocery store were just beginning to ready themselves for the long day ahead by moving and restocking food items on the shelves.

I got all of the food on my list except the fish. The fish was not on sale, so I decided after leaving the store that I would go to another—the same grocery store but at a different location. When I arrived at the store and made my way to the meat counter, another lady was standing there waiting for the butcher to return. She told me that the fish was on sale, and she too was waiting to buy some. As we continued to talk, I found out that she worked for this store but at a different location. When the butcher returned, she told us that there was only one box left. Out of kindness, the lady agreed to share the box with me. Her good will melted away the lousy feelings that I struggled with this morning. I did get my fish and a rain check should I need more. Talk about being in the right place at the right time.

Sometimes, we can see our foul moods lying in front of us, but still we have a difficult time stepping over or around them. In situations like this, we must take the focus away from ourselves and focus on God. God has a remedy for every situation.

Mystery

Sometimes, when I am involved in deep thinking, I will say out loud a part of my thought. Today is Friday, and I am alone in the house; my husband has gone to work, and my children are in school—finishing up their last year in high school. It snowed throughout the night, and it continues to snow, with the temperatures expected to get into the single digits.

The television is on, because it is my connection to the outside world. It allows me to relate to other unfamiliar voices when my inner thoughts become overwhelming. While speaking my thoughts out loud, I say the word "mystery," when a man's voice from television says the same word at the same time I do. How would you explain this occurrence?

Here

It is very important that my family and I sit down and have dinner together. I remember when I was growing up, my family and I ate dinner together. Sometimes we had a lot to say and at other times, not so much. After dinner, the kitchen closed unless one of us siblings had an afterschool activity. Having dinner with family is one way to nurture the family bond. Conversations are easier to have when family members are sitting next to each other. One evening, my family and I are sitting around the kitchen table eating dinner while the television plays in the background. As I am talking to my family, I use the word "here" and a lady's voice from television echoes the same word simultaneously. What are your thoughts?

An Agonizing Thought

For the past few days, I've had an uncomfortable thought and feeling of someone falling down on a knitting needle, piercing their chest. I tried very hard to dismiss this visual from my mind but could not completely erase it and would occasionally revisit it throughout the day. This morning as I am walking down the stairs, the thought grabs me again. About an hour later, while watching a morning talk show on television, the lady being interviewed begins to tell her story. She had fallen on a knitting needle, and it pierced her chest. "This is what I have been agonizing over," I said to myself as I continued to listen with amazement. After hearing of those events, my thoughts and feelings decreased in intensity each day until they soon vanished.

You Should Be Responsible for Something

Identify that which strengthens your resolve to do better.

This is an action-oriented world; change is constant, and it is the only action that will occur with or without our help. When you are born into this world, you are a world citizen and now have the right and responsibility to be an active participant. This is an undeniable right that is given from the Creator. Imagine being surrounded by a crowd and trying to move against the crowd to get to another place. To achieve this feat, you have to expend unbelievable energy. On the other hand, if you have no place in particular to go, following the crowd does not require any extra energy—just float along or drift with the crowd. Life is like this in that, ultimately, each one of us is responsible for whatever course we decide to take.

Although many of us have the willingness to do something, it will not sustain itself without having the skills, talents, and the passion. However, if we combine the willingness with the skills, talents, and the passion, we are looking at a path. Occasionally, I looked at some of the opening episodes of *American Idol*. Everyone who had an audition was willing, but one can clearly see who among them had the skills and talents. If you are willing but not quite sure you have the skills and talents, confide in someone you trust to give you an honest answer. And when you ask for an honest opinion, please be receptive. Should you have the willingness, passion, and commitment to grow and nurture your skills and talents, go for it! Plant your seed.

As you work to improve yourself, ask God to help you create and identify ways to use those skills and talents. There are many ways to express your creativity. For example, I can paint the walls in my house a different color to create a certain ambiance, or I can use paint to create a picture on canvas that will serve as a focal point on my wall.

How many ways can we use paint? The answer can only be found in you. Now, go out and paint!

Plant Your Seed

I'm going to plant this seed
And watch it grow.
I know because I believe
And my Father says so.

Each day, I'll get up –
Renewed, confident, and reassured,
Doing something no matter how small,
Pushing me closer to my goal.

I'll do what I can do for myself,
What I can't, I know God can.
Going beyond my limited understanding,
Revealing hidden paths to travel,
I'm taking a chance on me
In His will, these things will be.

Part 2
God Prepares the Way

Advantage

Try because it is an exercise that helps to maximize your potential.

To make my day special today, I popped some popcorn. Sometimes we have to do things that we do not do on a daily basis. Engage in an activity and make it special for you. As we become self-absorbed in problems, our energy level and mindfulness are absorbed, and we are left feeling numb, tired, and out of touch with our real lives. Have you ever had the experience of driving or riding in a car and being unable to recall any place or person you passed? To keep my thoughts in the moment, I deliberately observe people and places I pass and note something special about them. It could be the color of the clothing someone is wearing, how the person looks, or what they are doing. I instantly recall what I have seen when I arrive home.

Today, while I am writing down my thoughts as the radio plays in the background, I begin to write the word "advantage" in my journal. Suddenly a lady calls to the radio station and expresses her thoughts on the given topic and says the word "advantage" as I am writing it. By definition, the word "advantage" is very powerful. And when we keep our focus on God, despite everything going on around us, we have an advantage because victory is found in Him.

If we are seeking the advantage, we cannot allow ourselves to be taken hostage somewhere other than the present, because then we are not able to see the blessings that God surrounds us in. So stay present and alert.

An Observation

A darkened cloud passes in front
To let the sun out of the gate
Just then another cloud passes
And closes it until late.

The One

That which I watered grew faster.

I always knew that my husband was a special person. We met at a picnic while we were both attending graduate school at neighboring Midwestern states. I believe that our meeting was not by chance but one of design by God. Three months before I met my husband, I prayed and asked God to send me the right person. As I evaluated and looked back at some of the young men that crossed my path, none of them would I consider a possible mate. I needed help in that department. God says that we are to acknowledge Him in all things.

Sometimes, when our energy is channeled in too many different directions, we cannot fully see how important our mates are to us. It is only when our energy is controlled and focused that our lives become clearer, and we are able to see what is truly important.

When our children were younger, a great deal of our time and energy were spent making sure that they were financially, physically, and emotionally provided for. After our children left to attend college, I further realized how important my husband is to me. The rebalancing of our energies and time gave us more time to spend with each other. We were able to re-focus and share our hopes, dreams, and our ups and downs. I thank God for His blessings every day and for someone to share them with. For me, it is so much easier navigating through this world with someone you can depend on.

If you are tired of the do-it-yourself approach, contact God. He made you, so He knows who is best for you.

Our Own Oasis

Pushed all things aside,
So my husband and I
Went down to the waterside.

Randomly stacked rocks
Hiding what's below,
Only a few people know.

Climbing the rocks with care
An adventure itself to us,
Started out as a dare.

It wasn't enough to look
And stare across the blue horizon
Right there, now, just us two.

The waves teased us
As they crashed upon the shore,
Each time coming in more.

So we took off our shoes
And our socks removed,
Danced in and out.

Exhilarating and carefree fun
Being warmed by the sun,
Restored our souls and comforted our hearts.

We could have stayed all day
In our newly found oasis
Watching the boats sail away.

With a rock in hand
I dislodged from the sand,
We headed back
To where it all began

Forge Ahead

What brought the two together first?
What did you see?
What was it about the him or her
That sparked an interest so unique and new,
Culminating in a union, never before, just you two.

When problems come, and they usually do,
Think back no matter how far you travel
And revive the reasons why,
You selected—you allowed—him or her
To share that part in your heart,
A place of warmth, comfort, the two of you.

Visualize, then act to revitalize
The bond that existed for the very first time
As eyes met and time you did spend
Opened up a road—a path you willingly followed,
Reaching a point from atop you wed,
Visualize, then act and forge ahead.

Neighbor

A call some days to a friend that is far away restores the luster to a fading heart.

A few days ago, I got some mail from the mailbox and laid it on a wooden love seat in my kitchen. Today I decide to look through it and sort the bills from the junk. My favorite radio talk show is playing in the background. As I am standing over the recycle bin, I come to a letter with the general addressee label: "To the Neighbor." For some reason, I am fixated on the word "neighbor." As I put the letter into the bin, someone on the radio made reference to the word "neighbor."

That same day, I received an e-mail from my sister-in-law with an attachment. It was filled with inspirational stories, each with the theme, "This is where God wants you to be at this moment." All of the personal stories highlighted various occurrences that could have resulted in disaster for the people involved if they had not been where they were at that given time. This e-mail was ice cream on my cake. It further validated all of the occurrences that I had been experiencing; they were not coincidences. This is God's way of communicating to me that I am where I am supposed to be at this time. This e-mail was so powerful that I needed to share it with someone else. I did, by sending it to my best friend Mary. I can't wait for another message.

Are you sharing good stories with your neighbors and friends?

God Leads the Way

I am as light as a feather when I ride on the wings of the Lord.

"The Lord will make a way out of nowhere." My grandmother would always say this in response to something she or I hoped for. God always takes care of his children. I am reminded of how He guided the Israelites in the wilderness during biblical times.

Have you ever prayed for something after realizing that you did not have the means or the power to get it? Well, I have on countless occasions. Then sometime later, after you have forgotten about the request, that very thing shows up, better than you could have imagined it. All we have to do is believe and keep living a righteous life, because when we try to force things to happen, we make a mess. But when God works it out, it is such a natural and comfortable feeling.

I always wanted to visit New Orleans but could not figure out how to pay for the trip. During the summer of 2009, one of my husband's friends was getting married and wanted my husband to be a groomsman in the wedding. My husband and I made flight arrangements for our family to attend the wedding. We flew into New Orleans, spent a day, and drove to the location of the wedding.

God's blessings are many—so many that we cannot physically count them. God is the greatest!

Free to Soar

Do not allow others to pollute your pond.

I woke up this morning feeling inspired by the flight of birds. This may sound strange, but I am going to explain where the inspiration came from. Have you ever noticed what formation most birds fly in? If you have, then you know that birds form a V shape as they glide through the air. Why fly in the shape of a "V?" Well, I know there is a scientific explanation, but I would like to give this occurrence a spiritual explanation.

For me the "V" stands for victory as the birds freely move from here to there. They are provided for by the Almighty Spirit regardless of their destination. Are we, as God's children, expressing our victory? And are we carrying this attitude with us as we freely move about our daily lives? If we truly believe that we already have the victory because we rely on God to meet all of our needs, then there is no need to walk with our heads hanging down and feeling less than: we are free to soar. Continue to look toward the sky, and let the birds remind you that you indeed have the victory.

Victory

Up in the sky I see
Soaring directly above me,
Birds in flight
A marvelous sight,
A "V" formation,
God's confirmation.

Up in the sky I see
Soaring directly above me,
Birds in flight
A marvelous sight,
Flying in the formation "V,"
God's reminder,
I am free.

February 16th

Wow!

Last night, my husband and I were sitting in the living room watching television. We were engaged in a conversation when we both at the same time said the word "Wow!" It gets better. Someone from television, during a commercial, said "Wow!" at the same time we did. Can you offer an explanation for such an occurrence?

Artificial Barriers

Do not get burdened with troublesome thoughts. Pray and ask God for help as you ought.

We are constantly talking about the brown, the black, the yellow, and the white. What about the light? We have managed to divide, create lifestyles, engage in wars, kill, and breathe new life into hate on a daily basis because color motivates our actions. Biblically speaking, the essence of the Bible does not focus on the color of people. The focus is on how we are to treat each other as God has commanded.

How much would life change and what effects would it have on our lives—your life—if we could destroy the myths, remove but acknowledge the color, and interact with each other based on the intensity of the "light" that emanates from the body? This light, of course, is given to us by our Heavenly Father because we choose to believe, follow, and act on His truths. Having a beautiful light in our lives is so important, because it nourishes our bodies spiritually, mentally, physically, and can be a nourishing source and guiding light for others.

My Father's Eyes

In my Father's eyes
As He looks down
Upon us from high,
Sees no color,
Just His garden
Since the beginning of time.

In my Father's eyes
As he looks down
Upon us from high,
In a darkening world,

Searches for beacons of light
That radiates from the souls,
Fueled by His guiding words,
His sheep—His children.

In my Father's eyes
As He looks down
Upon us from high,
Continues to knock
Each and every day,
Some will and some won't
Open their hearts and minds
To true love, the Omnipotent One,
Through His eyes, at the very end, will decide.

Myths

What is this thing:
Having good hair?
Well, it's good to have hair.

What is this thing:
Skin color?
Well, it's good to have color.

What is this thing:
You're too old?
Well, to age is to be alive.

What is this thing:
Having too much or too little?
Well, you're precious in our Father's eyes.

Car Troubles

I can be as strong as I need to be, because the Lord is always with me.

We can spend a lot of time hanging out around the house alone, but when it is time to be around others, we have to venture out. And you will know that time because of a longing inside that pushes you toward action. So today, I left the house in search of human contact: I went to the mall. There I was able to fill my need. When I returned home and tried to put the car's gear in reverse, it would not move. I immediately called my husband. He came within twenty minutes and was able to dislodge the car's reverse gear. Moreover, I am so thankful that under His grace, God allowed me to get home without incident.

Another time that God provided safe passage for me and my family was when I started my drive from Iowa to South Carolina. I had just completed my required paperwork for my graduate degree. My brother, his family, and my mother had driven up the day before to accompany me on the drive. With all of my belongings stuffed in the back seat and hatchback of my yellow Plymouth Arrow, I started on the long road trip. We traveled a couple of hundred miles when my car started to sputter. The early evening had turned to late night, and something was definitely wrong with the car. As we entered Kentucky, the car would slow and then pick up speed sporadically.

It was early morning, and I was driving through the mountains that would lead me into the Smokey Mountains of Tennessee. I sputtered my way down, up, and around the challenging course. Through the darkness, I could see random sites of lights situated along and nestled into the mountainside. I prayed as I drove, and I drove as I prayed. It is hard to maneuver your way around the Great Smokey Mountains when your car is in excellent condition, so imagine my predicament. I prayed even harder when through my hatchback, I could only see the glaring headlights from semi-trucks. When the car slowed down, that was the time the semi-trucks got closer, and when the car sped up, I considered myself to be at a safe distance ahead of them.

Finally, when I saw the "Welcome to South Carolina" sign, I felt some relief because I had passed safely through the mountains, and I was almost home. After five to six more hours of driving, I pulled into my mother's driveway and parked the car. I tried to restart the car so my brother could check it out, but the car would not make a sound. It too had retired for the night.

God had granted me safe passage through the Smokey Mountains and dangerous roads, as He did for His children traveling through the Red Sea. What are your safe passage moments?

March 25th

Sunny

For days, I have been thinking about sending graduation invitations to family members and friends. In three months, my children will be graduating from high school. So today I decided that I would at least write the addresses on the envelopes. A commercial is on television and a lady says the word "sunny" just as I am about to write the word "sunny" on the envelope. What a beautiful word to brighten up a spring day.

The Simplest of Things

Give yourself and others the gift of motivation and not stagnation.

Just finishing a cup of tea, I went into the kitchen to wash out the cup, when I noticed two young squirrels playing on the deck. Two days earlier, I had turned two chairs and the table on the deck to their sides to prevent rain from accumulating on them. The squirrels were playing hide and seek, darting in, out, down, and over the chairs. It is amazing that from a simple action much enjoyment comes.

We have to use the example that the squirrels exhibit: create our fun and not rely on others to do this for us. And fun does not have to come with a high price tag. Look for the simple things to do that require little or no money, such as listening to music, dancing, painting, knitting, and walking.

God created the squirrels too, and on this day He used them to teach a lesson. So below, create your own list of fun things to do.

Create your fun list here (additional space at end of book):

How Does Your Garden Grow?

The Lord will send others who are in a better place to help us move beyond our current situation.

The weeds, grass, and leaves have all been removed. We have taken the hoe or tiller and chopped through the soil to reveal the dark chocolate soil hidden below. The fresh earthly aroma radiating from the soil overpowers you and awakens your soul to all of the possibilities. The heat from the sun sheds light into the dark spaces as the fresh air breezes across your skin. Even the birds are stirred to action as they browse the new soil for worms.

With careful selection and placement of each seed and plant, we dig the hole and cover them with soil, and we ask God for a bountiful harvest. Early in the morning before the sun reaches its peak, or maybe later in the evening, we water the fragile plants as they peek through the soil, never missing an opportunity to spy on our garden. As weeks turn into months, the once skimpy area transforms itself into a thick green space with blossoms and miniature fruit.

When we sow our seeds in daily relationships and interactions with others, it is important, I believe, to ask God for guidance and healthy developments. Just as we select our seeds for the garden very carefully, we have to use that care when we choose people. Do we carefully study people before we select or allow them into our lives? This is an important step, because the planting of some people into our lives can be an unhealthy addition, while others can bring enrichment. Keeping an eye on the relationships we form with people and how these relationships make us feel can help us determine whether to pluck the relationship or nourish it. The relationships that we choose to keep must be fed with nutrients that allow them to grow and strengthen.

For me, life is about growing with our roots spiritually based and sharing that knowledge with others to bring joy and improve the quality of others' lives. How does your garden grow?

March 28th

Scale

My son has a gift for drawing, and he has participated in various regional art shows over the years. This year he has drawn a scene that depicts a lighthouse anchored next to a cliff that overlooks the banks of a sea. A winding path leads up to the lighthouse, and it is surrounded by various plants. Off to the left of the lighthouse is the moon. As I am thinking about the moon and the scale of the moon to the size of the drawing, a man from television says the word "scale," using it in the same context as my thoughts.

Do we sometimes draw God to scale, thinking that some situations are beyond His control? He is all-powerful, all-knowing, and ever-present.

A State of Flux

When someone tries to give you smaller shoes to wear, leave them at their door.

When we cannot express our vision for our life in words or in writing, we need to spend some time praying, examining, and thinking about those things that have brought us joy in the past, those things that have transcended time and still bring our souls joy. So get started! If you never seek, you will never find. As I am writing this piece, the telephone rings; it is my daughter. She has just started the second semester of her freshman year at college. One of her goals for the new year was to be more assertive in her actions. Today, she told me that she had found a job on campus and was able to get additional hours of work after speaking with her employer. I could sense the excitement in her voice, and I know she could tell that I was excited as well. Had my daughter not taken the initiative to ask for additional hours from the employer, she would not have gotten them. In comparison, we also have to search for additional activities that keep our zest for life alive.

We have to quiet and reduce the thoughts in our minds that are self-defeating. By praying and asking God to help us, strength and clarity are brought to our thoughts. We cannot do this by ourselves. Also, we must make time during the course of our day to sit and think, and to receive an answer to our prayers. My grandmother use to say that if we make one step, God will make two. If our travels are in line with what God has for us, opportunities and people who can help us will surface. I remember wanting to attend graduate school after working three years after graduating from my undergraduate studies. I contacted my career counselor, Miss Zeigler, and informed her of my intentions. The same day that I called, she said that she would be meeting that week with an admissions recruiter who was looking for graduates that wanted to attend graduate school. The recruiter, on Miss Zeigler's advice, interviewed me through a telephone call, and the rest is history.

Today, begin to ask yourself honest questions and seek honest answers. Stop wasting your energy on useless thoughts and start using your energy to fuel thoughts that will move you toward a better way of life. To mark your progress in this area, test yourself: if you are able to express your desire for your life in a clear thought, orally or in written form, and it truly encompasses the essence of who you are, success is attainable. On the other hand, if you are having problems expressing your desires, continue to work on getting rid of all those negative thoughts.

I prefer to write down my vision, because then I can refer to it as many times as I want when I lose my momentum and when obstacles seek to deter me. My written statement, which has become my mission statement, falls in line with *Webster's Dictionary* definition: "a sending out or being sent out with authority to perform a special duty."

If we believe that God is with us and that it is on His authority that we go into the world to accomplish His predetermined goals, we cannot lose. Our lives are purposeful.

My Voice

When it's just me and my voice,
I sit still to listen
To the thoughts and ideas it brings,
My troubles uncovered,
My dreams revealed,
A true representation of who I am.

Imperfection

I'm not perfect—there's only one,
So if I make a mistake
don't be surprise,
I'm growing, learning, and becoming wiser.

April 20th

Coupons

    Standing in the kitchen and thinking about going to the grocery store, I am thinking that it would be nice if I had some coupons. At that time, a man from a television commercial says the word "coupons" as he continues to pitch the sale of mattresses.

    Thank God for giving His Son to pay for our sins. God's love is priceless, and we do not need to redeem a coupon to receive such an eternal gift. All we need to do is accept Him as our Lord and Savior, remain obedient, and acknowledge and ask for forgiveness when we sin.

Where's Your Joy?

Sometimes, you cannot take the road that is made by others; you have to create your own.

As we live our lives, there will often come times when we find ourselves needing a recharge—the times when we feel lethargic, unable to feel and find joy. What are you going to do? Yes, you! Well, just a suggestion: suck in the air and then execute. Do not overthink your situation, because it only strengthens your resolve to stay where you are. We have to move forward knowing that we have the strength because our spirit is rooted in God.

One night, I had a dream where I was a student at Princeton University. The professor took his physical education class onto an open field. He wanted to test his students' physical strength by having them run a race. I was at the back of the line, and my classmates were much younger than me. So you can see where this is going. However, when the professor gave us the go signal, I took off. I did not have time to think about how old I was in comparison to the other students or the fact that I might come in last because my younger counterparts would be faster. I just took off, and I found myself outrunning the rest of the class. I ran so fast that I lost everyone and couldn't find my way back to them because I was unfamiliar with the neighborhood.

Since I was separated from the rest of the class, I went back to my dorm and sat on the pillars surrounding the steps. A few minutes later, the professor with the rest of the class pulled up in the activity bus. They stopped by to see if I was safe. I thought that I might be penalized, but the professor said that it was okay because returning to the dorm was the best decision and the safest place to be.

When I woke up the next morning, this dream was still with me. I remembered the energy and drive I had. I had gone to some place different and participated in a new activity. I felt good! And these words became a part of my thought pattern: "Do something different. Get new energy!"

I then, in my conscious state, realized that up to that point, I had been operating in old energy, and it was pulling me down. Instantly, I decided to no longer stay around anything that has old, depressing energy, and that includes people or situations. Boredom is not my friend, and it should not be your friend either. Are you stuck in old energy?

The world is a beautiful place, and there are too many places to go and too many activities to enjoy. This is your world because you were born into it. Thank goodness this world does not exclusively belong to any one person or a select few. Whenever you find yourself getting discouraged and thinking happiness is for someone else and not you, remember that God created this world and allowed you to be present in it for a reason.

Now, become an activator and participant—get moving! When you need a little motivation, repeat the following thought that I introduced earlier: Do something different. Get new energy!

Not My Friend

I'd better get up from here
Boredom is creeping in,
And I can't do this again,
Boredom is not my friend.

It leaves me feeling useless
Taking away all of my dreams,
Lulling me into a senseless sleep
That deepens as time goes by.

Get up! Move! Do something!
Take that energy and redirect,
Establish a new path to travel and see,
There are so many things to do,
Some for you and some for me.

Pits

Do not engage with the wrong people.

Maneuvering around in this world is risky business, because you have to constantly avoid the ever-changing and constantly moving pits. These pits are filled with unhealthy activities and ideas that harm the body and the mind. So we have to be mindful and ask God for his guidance and strength that is needed to see and resist such temptations.

I remember as an undergraduate student living on the sixth floor in a dormitory. This floor was better known as "the penthouse." I soon found out why the floor was given that name. It was the partying floor. In the open area surrounding the individual rooms where the television and round table with chairs were located, girls would frequently gather, drink liquor, and smoke marijuana. Often, after returning to my room from class, I would see huge bottles of liquor surrounded by a thick cloud of smoke. Within a short period of time, the screams and the running up and down the hallway would start and last throughout the night. I would roll up my blanket into a log, put it next to the crack underneath my door to keep the smoke out, and open the window to let in fresh air.

After returning to my dormitory one evening and getting off the elevator, I could smell the smoke and hear the loud noises coming from the end of the hallway. As I quickly put my key into the keyhole to get into my room as fast as I could, a voice coming from the lobby said, "Come join us." I politely said, "No, thanks" and went hastily into my room. I thank God for giving me wise parents. My grandmother would always say, "You can get hooked up with the wrong people," and that gave me the strength to say "No, thanks."

How are you doing in this area? Do you have the strength to avoid people who would lead you down destructive paths?

April 29th

Cleaning

I am flipping through the pages of a magazine that I received in the mail, come to a page, and begin to read the title of the article. When I get to the word "cleaning," a voice from television says the same word at the exact time of my viewing.

Is there anything in your life that needs cleaning? Remember that God is able to wash away all of the dirt and filth that we may have accumulated over time, revealing a clean and renewed spirit within us.

Arrogance

God is at the beginning and the intersection of all of our opportunities and successes.

It takes a person with a strong inner spirit to admit when they are wrong and to admit that they do not know everything. And it takes an even stronger person to practice humility. When we are able to look at ourselves and identify our faults, we are well on the way to creating a better self. There is only one that is perfect and all-knowing.

Still, there are some people who think that they are perfect, that there is nothing in their being that needs to be changed. How many people do you know who transmit the attitude that says, "I know everything." Well, it is this type of thinking that becomes dangerous, and, moreover, evil if used as a weapon to quiet, berate, and oppress others.

When we think we know everything, God cannot use us for His purpose. We miss the opportunity to grow, but most of all, we miss a divine opportunity to get closer to God and to be used by Him.

So, let us change our hearts and our minds to reflect the goodness of God. Let us come into His presence with humbleness.

Follow Your Path

Never let your drive get up and go.

Your neighbor's ball is in your backyard. What do you do? Do you return the ball? Regardless of how you choose to handle this situation, a week later, your neighbor's ball is back in your yard. You return the ball, because you think that this is the neighborly thing to do. Two weeks pass, and when you walk around in your backyard, there it is again—your neighbor's ball. This time the ball has been thrown deeper into your backyard than on the previous times. So, returning the ball to your neighbor is going to require more of your energy. Imagine this type of behavior becoming more unpredictable and occurring more frequently. What would you do?

Sometimes we allow the problems of other people to become our own. We give them permission, at any time and level, to interrupt our path that God has uniquely designed for us. This is done because we constantly let others exhaust our resources, physically and mentally, to the point that we have nothing left. We should all be givers but not to the point that we are completely blown off of our course.

When the light within you shines bright and others know that you are going to someplace special, they will throw and continue to throw balls into your backyard. People who envy others' achievements have not identified, and are not moving toward, their life's mission. If they were, their maturity levels would not be infantile and evil in spirit. Moving on the right path requires faith, energy, and commitment. The lesson for us is to not envy what others are doing; just know that if it is possible for them, then it is possible for you.

Use your God-given skills and talents in a way that brings glory to God. Do not allow others to block your path to that special place that God wants to take you. Focus like you have never focused before.

Part 3
A Place in God's Hammock

AS CHILDREN OF GOD, WE ALWAYS HAVE A PLACE TO GO WHEN WE GROW WEARY, WHETHER AT HOME OR FAR AWAY. HE OFFERS US COMFORT, A PLACE TO GROW STRONGER IN OUR FAITH, AND A PLACE TO TACKLE THE PROBLEMS THAT ARISE IN DAILY LIVING.

An Angel from Above

There are some things that manifest themselves and cannot be explained, because they are unlike what we see and experience in the world in which we live.

In December 1986, I graduated from Iowa State University with a doctoral degree. I returned home after receiving my degree, because I had not yet landed a job. During that time, I constantly probed, prowled, followed up on job leads, and sent out numerous resumes. Despite my efforts, I did not get any job leads, and falling back into the same old routines that I had left behind was a growing and horrible thought. Besides this, I had left behind my significant other, who worked and lived in Omaha, Nebraska. Now, other men with wives and children and those without dreams had begun to send messages to me through people that I knew. They would make telephone calls to my mother's house and even had the nerve to stop by. I needed to get out of this madness!

As the days passed, and long summer days turned into short fall ones, my hope of finding a job was slowly disappearing; I lacked motivation. The stress continued to build, and it reached its highest point during one night in October 1987. That night, I decided to go to bed earlier than usual. Emotionally, I was beaten down, and going to sleep was the thing to do since there was nothing else to do. As I began to pray while kneeling on top of a twin bed, which was next to a window, I poured out my heart to God. When I opened my eyes and looked toward the heavens, suddenly, I saw an amazing sight: a spiraling, elliptical glow of beautiful light. This electric, amber, yellow, and white light floated softly down through the skies and landed in a patch of trees across the paved road. It reminded me of a dandelion seed floating through the air. With my eyes stretched wide opened, I jumped from my bed and ran into the den to get my mother. When we got back, the happening had ended. I knew that at that moment, I had experienced something that wasn't a natural part of the physical world in which I lived. God had sent me an angel to help me during this difficult time in my life.

I reflected on this happening constantly for weeks, and I still do. About two weeks later, I received a telephone call from a lady who I later came to know as Sharon. She wanted to interview me for a job, after having received my resume. After traveling to Omaha, Nebraska, and while interviewing for the position, the interviewer offered me the job. My motivation level surged, and I gladly accepted and thanked God for this gift. God sent His angel down from heaven to earth to open doors that I could not open. And this was the first of the two most important revered moments in my life.

Suddenly

Spiraling through the night air,
Feathering to the ground,
Amber and gentle electric sparks,
An answer to my prayer.

When your faith is in God, there are some things that defy an earthly explanation. These experiences have made my faith stronger and have placed me in a better place to help motivate and encourage others. Like many people, I have ridden the roller coaster into the valley of ups and downs but held on tight, because that's what roller coasters do. But I know that I have a constant companion. Although some of the turns in my life are not what I expected or could understand at that moment, I understand that these turns were what I needed, because they were all a part of the plan that God has for my life.

So when you feel as if you might be thrown from the roller coaster, hold on! You, too, have a constant companion: one who loves you and is able to take care of you whether you're on a straight path or going around the bend.

Motivation

I am motivated by others' success
Able to see the obstacles pushed out of their way,
A clearer path to travel down
Anticipating and expecting a better day.

My life mirrored by parts of theirs
Enough to move me beyond self-imposed borders,
A road that knows no boundaries,
Success, failure, I can now bear.

So I'm thankful when others succeed,
Better yet, it's those that I seek
To radiate a once darken place,
And uncover the things that I'm yet to face.

Hyper Spirituality

Lord, help us to be righteous and not self-righteous.

People who initiate a search to develop and reach their spiritual self are indeed rich. I believe that it is extremely important to understand that developing the spiritual self is a process, and we never get to sit on the top of the mountain, feet dangling and sighing. Our journey is meant to be shared with others: encouraging, motivating, and performing acts of kindness, emitting such a light that others will see God through us. Jesus says in Matthew 5:16: "Let your light so shine before men, that they may see your good works, and glorify your Father which is in heaven."

From the paths that I have traveled in this world, I have noticed that some people wear the persona that they have reached the top and therefore are more qualified to look down, criticize, and judge others. These people want to give others the impression that they are more spiritual, wiser, and more religious than other believers. People with this type of attitude selfishly claim God for themselves and are unwilling to share Him with others. And thanks goes to God because His son died for all of our sins.

For example, I have been around many churchgoing people who feel that God will only speak to and act on the behalf of ministers. So they ask their ministers to pray for them. These members have slowly given away their powers while continuing to elevate their pastors to a level that is only reserved for God. Man is man, and God is supreme.

Each day there is something that we can all work on to make our light shine much brighter. God is available to all, and within His grace we can approach His throne through prayer.

June 1st

Mary Williams

I was working on the computer when the telephone rang, and my husband answered. It was my friend Mary Williams. My husband told her that I would call her back. I did call at a later time, but she was not at home, so I left a message. While I was eating a late lunch at the kitchen counter, the telephone rang again. I hurriedly ran over to pick up, thinking it was my friend returning my call. It was not my friend, but the lady identified herself as Mary Williams. She was asking for donations for a local charity. No coincidence here!

Bring It to the Light

When you know the truth, it will make you stronger. When you're wrapped up in a lie, it won't survive.

We have to be bold and strong in the Lord as we go through each day and deal with others who may not be rooted in God's teachings. With the knowledge that God is always with us, we must stand up and speak up when a wrong is being committed. I have seen people embark on their spiritual journey only to return to their pre-journey ways. Some people become weaker and more timid instead of growing in their faith. God is a God of action. He needs strong soldiers that are willing to confront difficult challenges. We must humble ourselves before God and stand with the power and strength that He has given us to effectively handle problems that arise from our daily interactions with others. We must also look for ways to help others who are in need of spiritual growth.

I remember going into a deli to pick up some sandwiches for lunch. I ordered four sandwiches, and when they had been made, a young man brought them and laid them on the front counter. I got up from where I was sitting and went over to the counter and paid for the sandwiches. I was still standing and waiting for the young man to put the sandwiches in a bag. He did not, and he proceeded to take the order of the next person in line. So I asked him for a bag, and he looked at me with a puzzled expression on his face.

The lady standing behind the person that the young man is now serving says, "Give her a bag." She did not have to say anything, but in her boldness, strength, and stance for what is right, she did. I appreciated her concern, but I too needed to stand in my boldness and strength for what was right in this situation.

We must also teach our children to stand in their boldness and strength, which are given to them through our God. Age is not an indicator of wisdom or lack of it; we have to observe the actions of others to determine their wisdom and intentions. And regardless if the wrong is being committed by an adult or by someone else, speak up, tell, and keep telling until someone listens.

In the Lord

I'm alive in the Lord
As I look around and above.
Green pastures, calm waters,
I can stand in his love.

I'm alive in the Lord
When I marvel at his works,
The position of the sun, moon and stars
To lighten the darken skies,
Made by him who sits on high.
A helping hand that reaches down,
And guides us and carries us through
Uncertain and challenging times,
He firmly attaches our feet to the ground.

July 2nd

Popsicle

Throughout the year, the grocery store where my family shops gives customers coupons after their purchases, which can be redeemed either for a gift card or a card that can be used to purchase gas at a service station. So this morning, I counted the coupons to see how many I had. I then decided to look at the rest of the coupons lying atop the microwave. I was particularly drawn to a coupon that advertised fruit popsicles. The thought of popsicles in fruity flavors of strawberry, cherry, and banana was refreshing, and as I contemplated the ideal of purchasing a box on my next visit to the grocery store, a woman's voice from a television commercial says the word "popsicle."

Unlike the temporary sensation of eating a popsicle, the Lord is able to continuously renew our outlook on old or new problems and to rekindle positive attitudes toward life. He is able to replenish all of the nutrients that we need to grow our spiritual self.

So let go of anything that would seek to stale or defile your spirit and look to God for permanent refreshment.

Experience

Stop!
Look!
There's a dragonfly fluttering across the pond,
Minnows dancing along the water's edge,
A swan cruising up and down,
Ducks bobbing for finds below
and chirping birds with surround sounds.

Feel!
The soothing comfort of warm pavement
The sensation of toasty grains of sand under your feet,

Memories brought back from when you were a child,
Sending jolts of energy throughout the body
that allow you to breathe a sigh of sweet relief.

Engage!
Go out no matter where you roam—
A thousand miles, a hundred, or just one,
In search of anything that stirs the soul,
Bringing contentment and peace within,
Giving us back what God intended.

Composure

There are days when my soul is in need of recharging
'Cause I drag about with purpose low,
Moving away from the light that inspires,
The light that guides me on my path
to that something: I must get back on track.

God understands that in my mortal self,
I will from time to time weaken,
That's when HE manifests his will
through things I hear or see,
To bring me back to the course HE'S set
with strength, wisdom, and all things best.

July 19th

Weariness

It was midweek, and my husband sensed that something was bothering me. I told him that I felt weary. That morning at church, the pastor's sermon said that we should not be weary. We should continue to trust in God with everything we have. God will take our burdens.

Once an Enemy, Now My Friend

A God of justice who comforts the restless soul.

My mind reflects on the period when my job came to an end, back in June 2007. The first few days at home were okay; I figured I would use that time to rest. A month later, I was still okay, because I had hope that I would find another job soon. I was furthered encouraged by the fact that my education would help to catapult me into another job. As the rest of the months passed, so did my hope. I applied for many jobs without the success of getting many interviews, except for two. Currently, as I write this story, I am still unemployed, but my hope of finding work that matches my skills and talents is higher than ever.

The times that follow a layoff, seen or unforeseen, is normally mired in anger, frustration, disappointment, hopelessness, and many other feelings. There are some days when you feel that you have reconciled with your current circumstances, and the next hour or day, you walk around feeling miserable. It seems like you are in a race, but anywhere along the route someone can pull you and make you start the race all over again. The unpredictable feelings surrounding unemployment can lead you down a road of despair, a feeling that is contagious and has a powerful effect on those closest to you. I know because there were many days that I traveled this road.

Over the two and a half years of unemployment, I was faced with managing my free time. Looking in the face of free time every day was a scary thing to do. Besides looking for a job, I constantly wrestled with the thoughts of how I would manage boredom when it visited again. This frenzy was leading me into a state of fear. However, I continued to read my Bible and focused on the scriptures that spoke of fear not being from God. I would use this as ammunition against evil thoughts that came at me on a daily basis, and I cherished the support that I got from my husband and family.

Throughout my free time, God was able to communicate with me. With the persistent gifts of knocks, I knew God had something else He wanted me to do. He was answering my prayers, because I had prayed before my job ended that He would guide me to a path that would allow me to use all of the skills and talents that He had given me. So I began to write about my experiences with the sincere hope of inspiring others along their path.

Time, once an enemy, had become my friend.

July 21st

Arm & Hammer Baking Soda

I poured some baking soda down the garbage disposal because there was an odor that would periodically surface. I warmed my tea and left the kitchen to go into the living room. From there, I settled in to watch television. One commercial went off, and another followed. While watching a commercial, sections from unrelated commercials intermingled with the one showing, and for a short period of time an image of a box of Arm & Hammer Baking Soda, the same size and brand that I poured down the garbage disposal, flashed on the screen.

God is also in the cleaning business, yielding better results than Arm & Hammer Baking Soda. No matter what we have done in the past, how dirty we have gotten, He can give us a clean spirit, a spirit that leads us into eternity, and one that He can use to touch people around us.

Should any one of us need cleaning at any given time, he or she should contact God.

July 24th

Judy

For a couple of days, I had been thinking about some of the people and friends that I grew up with—some in my neighborhood, and some that I went to school with. One that I could not get out of my mind was Judy, who died of cancer in her forties. We attended the same elementary, high school, and college. Around ten thirty this morning, I saw two women walking up my neighbor's driveway. I had seen a car driving along the street minutes before, because it was moving suspiciously slow, and that caught my attention. They were Jehovah's Witnesses. A minute later, my doorbell rang. It was one of the ladies that I saw walking up my neighbor's driveway. I opened the door and she greeted me. She wanted to know my name, and then she told me that her name was Judy.

Some things may be coincidences, but there are some occurrences that you innately know have divine guidance.

July 26th

Confirmation

It rained earlier this morning, so the sky is still cloudy. Contrary to the dreary sky, the temperature is expected to fluctuate between the high seventies to early eighties. Today, I needed to go to the bank, and so I did; on the way back I stopped by Walgreen's. At the checkout counter, a man was standing in front of me. He looked at me and asked did I operate a school. I told him yes. He, too, was operating a school. Continuing, he said that he had recognized me from meetings we had attended. He went on to tell me that he was closing his school because of the accountability issues from the state; they were causing monetary hardships on the school. I had closed my school two years earlier for the same reasons. After hearing this, I felt more at ease about making the decision to close my school.

God's confirmation was a welcome gift.

An Airport Vendor

As you carefully make and execute plans, allow room for the God factor.

While traveling to attend a wedding in Alabama, the same wedding I talked about in an earlier story, my family and I had to change airplanes in St. Louis, Missouri. So I went into one of the stores to buy a magazine and a pack of gum. I also bought a copy of Oprah's *O Magazine* to read during our route. The young man standing at the checkout counter said he did not know that Oprah had a magazine. He went on to tell me that he enjoys writing and was thinking about writing a book. At that moment, I felt a connection to this would-be author, because I too was in the process of organizing my thoughts to begin writing my book. And from this momentary kinship, I encouraged him to continue with his writing and to complete his book.

Two hours earlier as the plane was lining up on the runway, readying itself for takeoff, I had asked God to give me a sign and the inspiration to write a book if indeed this was the direction He wanted my life to take. And after talking to this young man at the airport, I recognized that this was the sign and that I needed to do what I had encouraged the young man to do: write a book!

Through a casual conversation with this young man standing at the store's counter, I was energized to continue my writing. God had used this young man and me as vessels whose purpose was to encourage each other. God is amazing!

July 28th

Shirley

Last night, I had a dream about one of my high school friends. Her name is Shirley. I have not seen or heard from her since our early twenties. I was thinking about her, wondering where she is, and how she is doing while watching one of the shows that I look at during the morning. The host then introduces her guest, and can you guess her first name? Yes, it is Shirley.

Is this a mere coincidence, or is this something greater?

The Lure of Fame and Riches

I may not have anything, but I have everything in God.

Sometimes, it seems like some people prefer to walk on their heads, in that the traditional concepts and ways of operation have reversed. The acts that used to be bad are now considered good, and the good is something that is to be challenged and frowned upon.

We are constantly reminded of this reversal of traditional thoughts and deeds by the stories of people featured on the news, radio, Internet, magazines, and locally through our neighborhood gossip. For instance, the bad behavior of people is validated as appropriate behavior with monetary rewards and visual recognition. And as this process continues, it takes on an appearance of normality. For example, some people are verbally and physically abusive to others, while some lie and take advantage of other people.

Some people are so hungry for fame that they will do whatever it takes to get there: the uglier, the more fame and money. Be that as it may, we are taught through biblical scriptures that as we see people prospering from bad behavior, we should go on about our business because these people will have their rewards. And Jesus further states in Mark 4:19: "And the cares of this world, and the deceitfulness of riches, and the lusts of other things entering in, choke the word, and it becometh unfruitful."

No one is perfect, but we cannot continue to deliberately pick God up and put Him down in order to fulfill our selfish needs without expecting some consequences. God is not a toy. In Luke 12:5, Jesus is speaking to his disciples as many people gather: "But I will forewarn you whom ye shall fear: Fear him, which after he hath killed hath power to cast into hell: yea, I say unto you, Fear him."

So today, I ask you, "Does your nay mean nay, and does your yea mean yea?"

Part 4
The Blackboard is Everywhere

Learning Without Walls

We can cross borders and face things unknown, but in Christ, we know that we are never alone.

When we truly believe that God reigns in Heaven and on Earth, we have an endless supply of wealth. Should we fall to the temptations of things, we can regain our composure by asking for God's help. Many of us stockpile items to temporarily feel good—by tomorrow, we have gone on to something else. We are blessed when we have good health (taking into consideration our genes and the mindful sense to avoid things that are contrary to God's teachings), a place to stay, food to eat, clothes to wear, and people who love us. Because God knows what we need at all times and He delivers, we are wealthy—maybe not by the world's definition of wealth, but one defined spiritually.

Some people buckle when they become overwhelmed by the pressures of society, and they need help from others to escape evil's demoralizing claws. This takes me back to the time when my husband and I were looking around Campus Common in downtown Ithaca, New York. There a certain young man caught our attention:

Not Far Away

While touring the area,
An ivy leaf college town,
A young man dressed in black
Pants, shirt and shoes,
A rainbow cap with a hanging tassel,
Caught our sight.

As we stopped obeying the light,
A great big bus with the right of way,
Could not go 'cause it yield to,

The man in black and another attached,
Crossing the walkway without a thought.

A car came out and we took its spot,
Along a busy street near campus common,
Fed the meter and started our walk,
Browsing the shops for things unique,
An African, Indian, and souvenir store.

The man in black we saw again
As we made our way back,
A young man oblivious to those around,
Eating something he held in his hand,
And actively searching for more.

No interactions with others around,
He continued to search in all the cans,
Pulling out a piece of bread,
Then moving to the next,
Thoroughly enjoying what he had found.

A city known, a college known for intellectual thinkers
An aura of worth and self-development,
People indoctrinated in the college's tradition,
A young man roams the street,
In search of something to eat.

A Surrounding View

The next day of our stay in Ithaca, my husband and I drove a couple of miles to visit a park, which included a waterfall, while our children were still on campus completing their college tour. The view along the way was refreshing and calming to our souls. On our drive to the park, one thing that was different from what I normally see in Wisconsin was the location of the mailboxes and homes. Mailboxes lined the road, and that was the only way we could tell someone lived there. The houses were built deep into the hillside.

Those of us who are in tune with our inner selves can feel when we need to nourish our souls, and often we do this by seeking out the pleasures that link us back to God—in this case, a waterfall:

Solace

Surrounded by auburn and gold lit trees,
We trampled over crunchy leaves and assorted rocks
To reach the base of a protective cove
That shelters a beautiful waterfall.

Watching everything as we ventured through,
Our eyes never had cast
Upon the view that lay before,
Excited, renewed, in awe we went.

Uncovered earth from side to side,
Hard and soft stone all in their place,
An ascending sight from where we stood,
Challenged over time by weather worn.

Black and gray remnants at the foot of the mountains
Paved the path with leaves as cover,
A meandering way around and about,
Cozy and quiet, a private getaway.

Alone, coupled, or one with friends,
A combination seen along the illuminated route,
A friendly smile and a slight hello
To those who would pass them by.

I heard before I could see,
The mighty roar of the waterfall
Thunderously pouring into the basin just below,
Nature's own remedy for those who thirst and dare to go.

Off to College

It is the darkest when the lights are first cut off, but it brightens with the passage of time.

My husband and I took our children to New York for their first year of college. It took about thirteen hours to get there by car, but it wasn't a bad drive. There were many scenic sites: cities like Cleveland and Buffalo, which we passed through but we had never visited before, a view of Lake Erie, and a look at the mountains.

After spending some time on the beautiful campus of Cornell University, my husband had to return home to take care of some family business. So while driving from Ithaca to Syracuse to take him to the airport, I began to write down his travel itinerary. As I was writing the letters "P.M.," a man's voice from the radio said "P.M." at the same time of my writing. By now, I know that these precise moments are not by chance. God can communicate with us anywhere and when He wants to.

After my husband left, I started to feel a little overwhelmed, because I needed to make sure the financial and living arrangement were taken care of for my son and for my daughter when she enrolled in Syracuse University the following week. In the forefront of my mind, I kept repeating, "The Lord is with me wherever I go." I have a plaque of those exact words, which stands next to our family Bible at home. I still felt tired but was now confident that everything was going to work out, and it did.

God's promise that He will be with us always is all that we need to carry our tired bodies through whatever trials we may encounter.

October 4th

Lessons Learned from Animals

Create melodies and share them with the world.

It is early fall, and cool air has arrived. As a result, the big black walnut tree in my front yard has lost most of its leaves. A few leaves with yellow and brown spots are scattered across the yard, and the huge limbs that were once loaded with walnuts are almost bare. The squirrels, in the meantime, have collected most of the walnuts from the ground, and they now continuously scale the tree to find the leftovers. They scurry up and down the tree with one or two walnuts jammed into their mouths throughout the day, and repeat the same routine early each morning. Have you ever wondered why God created squirrels? Maybe God created squirrels to show us that working together can help everyone.

One day as I am searching the web on the computer, I hear a plopping noise coming from the front yard. At that time, my husband walks through the front door and says, "The squirrels are having a good time, taking the last of the walnuts." Until this time, I had not gathered any walnuts for myself. So I run outside to see what is going on. With amazement, I watch the baby squirrel jump from limb to limb, chewing away at the stems of the walnuts until they drop to the ground. As the walnuts fall, the two adult squirrels then skate across the yard, collect them, and carry them across the road to bury them in their secret places. I, too, quickly gathered a few for myself and stashed them inside the house.

The squirrels had figured out a system in which they worked together to accomplish their goal: getting and maximizing their winter supply of walnuts. Every time I think about these squirrels, I shake my head, smile in awe, and ask myself, "Why can't more people work together for common causes?"

We can all learn from the behavior of the squirrels. If we would only use the skills and talents that the Lord has given us to work with others, we could accomplish great things.

The Rabbit and the Blackbird

Aim to stay above the fray on each God-given day.

I'm sitting in my wooden chair at the kitchen table and brainstorming some ideas. I look down at the garden, which is now covered with dry leaves and surrounded by a somewhat dismantled fence, and see a big blackbird sitting on the neighbor's fence. Below, a rabbit sits staring at the bird; they continue to stare at each other for a minute or two.

Suddenly, the blackbird flies to the opposite end of the fence and perches. The rabbit runs in that direction too. Standing up on its hind legs with pointed ears, the rabbit continues to look at the bird. This lasts for a couple of minutes until the blackbird flies away, leaving the rabbit to figure out how to get to the outside of the enclosed fence.

Twenty to twenty-five minutes later, the blackbird returns, with flapping wings, gliding through the air over the garden. This time it sits atop a skinny wooden fencepost. Out of nowhere the rabbit appears, hopping and jumping into the garden and staring at the bird. Thirty seconds later, the blackbird flies away into our neighbor's backyard while the rabbit watches.

Two hours later, I see the rabbit chasing the blackbird around my backyard until it again flies into my neighbor's backyard. The rabbit continues to hop around, but the blackbird is nowhere to be seen. Finally, the rabbit nestles itself between a line of tall hedges that separate my yard from the neighbors' to the left, waiting patiently for the blackbird's return. The blackbird does return, but this time it sits on an electrical line above the garden. The rabbit looks at the blackbird, but it does not move.

Eventually, the blackbird flies to one huge tree, then to another in my neighbor's backyard, returns, and lands back onto the electrical line. The rabbit continues to watch but does not move from where it is still sitting, underneath the hedges. The blackbird soon flies away and never returns, while the rabbit too disappears from my sight.

The relationship between the blackbird and the rabbit is a confusing one. Were they engaged in friendly play, or were they involved in a game of survival? How many of our relationships are confusing?

Let us pray to ask God for help in discerning our relationships with people. And if we do, as time passes, He will give us clarity so that we are able to see the other person's true motivation within our relationships.

Unusual Events Require Unusual Actions

Beliefs should elevate and not deflate.

In our black 2003 Saturn, my daughter and I begin to cruise down the highway, first traveling through unfamiliar roads that connect one city to another until we finally get to Interstate 81. We are riding on four wheels with only three hubcaps. The missing hubcap flew off somewhere between Milwaukee, Wisconsin, and Ithaca, New York. We almost lost a second hubcap in Ithaca when we turned the corner of a downtown street, and the hubcap rolled onto it. My husband, daughter, son, and I had no idea of this incident until a lady brought it to our attention by waving her hands and yelling from her car in the back of us. Then a man graciously brought the hub cap to us as we waited in a nearby parking lot. The wheel with the missing hubcap became known as our badge of honor. It represented the many miles we had traveled to reach our destination.

We continue our ride down Interstate 81 without the presence of the rest of our family. My son had just been enrolled in college and now lived on campus. And my husband had returned home the day before. I am comforted, because I know that God is traveling with us. He's real. With that assurance, my daughter and I continue the drive.

Before getting the luggage out of the car, I go into the motel to confirm our arrival. The lady at the front desk is very cordial; it's good to see a smiling face and hear a helpful voice when you're so far away from home. As she prepares the paperwork, she tells me, as another resident listens nearby, that recently the motel housed a husband and wife who were involved in a serious accident on Interstate 81. Their car was destroyed, and they appeared to be badly bruised but didn't suffer any serious health injuries. As the desk clerk continues her conversation, she says that the couple had been traveling with their dog. And although the motel doesn't house animals, it did so in this particular case. Unusual events require unusual actions.

Imagine the billions of creative minds that God has created in this world, each with its own unique talents and skills. Think about all of the times that you had to use a creative approach to solve an unexpected problem. You are creative because you were made by the Master Artist and Creator: God, the Maker of Heaven and Earth.

I encourage you to embark on a journey to discover all of the innate goodies that God has blessed you with and to share them with the world.

He's Real

When we're slow 'cause we don't know where to go,
That's the time we must realize,
There's One who's close by
And hears us when we cry.

Retreat inwardly and find the strength,
Tear down walls and things that destroy,
Look toward the sky when you call,
He's there and won't let us fall.

This is the time to redefine
Who you really and truly are,
No pretense, let it be real,
A new beginning and you revealed.

God can and yes He will,
Take care of you and your needs,
Look toward the sky when you call,
Peace, tranquility—your heart He'll fill.

September 26th

Colors

Since the arrival of fall, I have been thinking about all the wonderful colors—special ones created by God that revive our senses and thoughts. This is one of my favorite seasons. This morning, I am looking at a cooking show where the chef's specialty is cooking Spanish dishes. My mind is still focused on the many colors displayed during the fall season, but for some reason the color orange takes precedence over all the others. Mentally, I'm thinking of the word "colors" when the chef uses the same word to describe the variety of vegetables he used to create his dishes.

A Change in Season

Pastel orange sherbet popsicles
Towering over emerald ones,
A view to see from my window
As I stare across the backyard,
All standing in a separate row.

It's that time of the year again
Such beauty for the eyes to behold,
A range of hues from top to bottom
Waving wildly as the wind passes by,
But still standing tall and bold.

A mellow shadow cast over all beneath,
Retreat from worries that rob the soul
Full of hope, joy and calm
To face the things that disturb the water
And makes us move beyond our wall,
Hooray! Hooray! Hooray for fall!

A Church Appearance

Feed your mind the seeds you want it to sow.

Last night, I had a dream in which I suddenly found myself in a bathroom inside a church. I was at the church to attend my cousin's wedding and needed to go to the bathroom before the ceremony started. After using the bathroom (a no-no while you're sleeping), I looked over my shoulder, and there appeared without any warning a small black dog with patches of white hair on its ears. I was standing there looking at it with a puzzled face, trying to figure out why it was there and staring at me.

In the morning, around eight, my husband and I went for a walk around the neighborhood. Walking helps us clear our minds and brings clarity to current problems and situations. During the walk, I told my husband about the strange dream I had last night. We talked, and at times laughed about how dreams have no physical limitations—how dreams can be rational, irrational, or a mixture of both.

Later that day, after cooking dinner, I took a break to read a magazine. I was eager to read the one that I had received earlier during the week. So I went out on the front porch and began to leisurely read. As I neared the end of the magazine, slowly turning the page, a picture caught my attention. Looking closely at the picture, I could see a lady sitting at her desk and a small dog also sitting on the desk next to a laptop. It wasn't just any dog. It was the dog that I saw in my dream. I jumped from my chair, ran into the house, and showed my husband the picture, pointing to the dog and explaining to him that this is the same dog I saw in my dream.

Underneath the picture, the article gave information about how the lady in the picture published her book. This story motivated me to continue with my writing, and it further confirmed that when we need that extra push and motivation to complete projects, God will deliver.

What projects are you currently working on? Do you need inspiration? Then ask God to guide you and to confirm whether your thoughts and actions align with His wishes for you.

Use What You Have

When you bow down to the pressures from others, you might just find, on your way up, that you're all alone. However, if you do what is right, God will always be by your side.

    I woke up this morning to a windy, cloudy, and wet day. Trying to get motivated for a day of writing, I went to the back of the house, where I could hear the chimes: one with a bass and the other, a soprano sound. I poured myself a cup of tea and a bowl of soup, and went into the living room. From the window, I heard the roaring of the wind as it moved through the trees. My attention was interrupted when I heard an amazing story coming from one of the early morning television shows. The story was about a young Malawian man who built a windmill that provides the energy needed to produce light for his family and his village. What was more amazing is that he learned the mechanics by reading books from the library. Before constructing the windmill, his siblings had to read by candlelight. Despite the naysayers who ridiculed him while he built the windmill, he did not stop.

    This young man did not let what he did not have prevent him from realizing his dream. We should all strive to be like him. Some of us have plenty of, some less of, some too much of, and yet we are still unable to figure out how to realize our dreams. It is during these times of uncertainty that we must ask God to show us how to use the things that He has blessed us with to move beyond our current circumstances. As a result of the young Malawian man's determination, persistence, and goodwill, he was given the opportunity to attend college and now has a bright future. So do many of the people who live across the African continent.

    When we help others, we help ourselves. But most of all, we remain obedient to the word of God when He says that we should love our neighbors as we love ourselves.

A Good Samaritan

Change your ways before showing others the way.

After an early Sunday walk, my husband and I went to Menard's, which is a home improvement store, to buy some screens for our gutters, in hopes that they would keep the leaves and other debris out, allowing for the easy flow of rain and melting snow. We had selected some screens that were on sale, and they were much cheaper than the others that were also on sale. We were feeling confident that we had made the right decision and had meticulously counted the correct number that we needed and had loaded them in our cart.

Still standing there and almost ready to leave, a man approached us and started talking. He explained that last year he had bought the same screens that we were about to buy, and they did not work; the open holes would allow enough debris to enter and still clog the gutters, preventing the flow of water. He went on to say that earlier during the year he replaced the old screens with the ones that cost a little more, and they worked. We thanked him for his advice and bought the screens that he suggested.

Coming from a good place in his heart, this stranger freely gave us helpful advice. He could have just looked at us and kept moving. My husband and I knew that God had sent him in our direction. This was perfect timing. Would you have done what this man did?

God watches over those who seek His advice in all situations. If we cannot help someone, then definitely do no harm.

☙❧

Part 5
Absorbed in the Light

A Pick From Nature

A God of beauty who comforts the restless soul.

Today, my husband and I went to pick apples during the afternoon. If you want some immediate relief from thinking about all of your troubles, visit your local farmer's apple orchard and pick the apples yourself. The amazing colors—maroon, crimson, ruby, yellow, and all colors in between—are breathtaking. Furthermore, the openness of the field and the circulation of fresh air is a natural therapy session. Not only do the apples provide nutrients to the body but also nourishment to the soul. An apple is a fruit of beauty, because it represents one of the natural gifts given to us by God and is sustained by His continuing gifts of air, sun, water, and earth.

You can pick any fruit or vegetable—they all come from the same source: God.

Designer Threads

Lord, I am going to seek, and please let me find, what is under your will and perfect design.

In a dream last night, I found myself inside a shopping mall. As I walked through the doors into the mall, a dress on display caught my attention. While staring at this dress, a saleslady walked up to me and asked if I was interested in trying it on. The dress was beautiful—dressy and sassy. I was fixated on the look of the material. The rich earth tone colors of dark chocolate and beige intermingled with the color white, creating an unusual pattern and look.

That afternoon, while looking through a magazine, I came to a page where I saw a model wearing a designer dress with the same material that the dress was made from in my dream. How unusual is this?

Ducks?

In our dreams, everything is possible. The dream I had last night was about a duck wearing a hat—but not just any hat, my blue hat, and I wanted it back. I would normally grab this hat just before heading outside during the winter months. There it was floating on the water. Every time I thought that the duck would come ashore or come close enough to the edge so that I could snatch my hat from its head, it would swim back to the middle of the pond. The duck stayed beyond my reach.

I do not have an answer for this one. Do you?

For Me

A glowing figure under the tree
Standing there just for me,
God's way of letting me know
That He's always there and would be.

Pure Light

In 2006, I found myself going through a very stressful period. I had to close the school that I opened in August 1998. Over the nine years of its operation, there had been many obstacles threatening the success of the school, but through perseverance and God's grace, the school continued. Many of the problems were mandates handed down to private schools that participated in the School Choice program, a state-funded program that allows parent to send their children to private schools. Large sums of money were often needed to implement these changes, and the mandates could surface any time during the school year.

After many long and difficult weeks at school during the school's last year of existence, I was compelled to take a walk on a Saturday afternoon. I needed to get out of the house and wrestle with my thoughts. Before leaving home, I prayed and asked God to guide me through the transition of closing the school. I also remember asking God during my confusion if He had abandoned me. I was feeling alone and had many unanswered questions about closing the school. Is closing the school the right thing to do? If so, what would I do since my job would also come to an end, and how long will it take before I get another job? If not, what can I do to raise the necessary funds to keep the school open?

As I walked along the tree-lined street of orange, yellow, auburn, and golden leaves, I continued to pray and tried desperately to make sense of my senseless thoughts on a cool but sunny day. Well, I walked for about a mile, passing the elementary school and Town Hall, crossing a major street, and viewing the Milwaukee River Waterfall.

My mind was clearing as I continued my walk. As I walked along a little path next to a wooded area, I heard the rustling of leaves. I stopped to see what could be making such a ruckus. I did not see anything in the area, but as I looked further into the forest, I did. There it was—AN UNBELIEVABLE SIGHT! Standing under an extended branch of a tree was a glowing figure. The image was made of pure glowing light. It was not the kind of light that you can see through. Furthermore, I did not see any human physical features such as arms, legs, or other body parts. But the top part of the form was smaller than the rest of its shape. It kept glowing—a living glow. I wasn't frightened; in fact, I felt a special connection to it. The sight of this angelic being was like the feeling that you get when a relative (someone who you enjoy seeing) pays a surprising visit. So I stood there blinking my eyes to see if I was seeing things, but it did not move. For as long as I wanted to look, it remained. I stayed there staring until I came to the realization that what I was staring at was not from this world. I knew it was an angel. Finally, I walked off slowly, looking back to see if the image was still there—and it was. It stayed there until I moved out of view. As I kept walking, I kept replaying in my mind what I had just seen. My once weakened composure became stronger.

God had sent me another Angel to let me know that He was still there and would be there for me throughout time. God is always there with us when trouble comes and will help us make adjustments and decisions as needed. We only need to ask and open up our hearts. God's ways are not like our ways and therefore cannot be explained by using our definitions.

Today, whenever I read scriptures that make reference to light, I have a deeper understanding of its meaning. For example, in Genesis 1:3: "And God said, Let there be light: and there was light" and when Jesus says, "I am the light of the world: he that followeth me shall not walk in darkness, but shall have the light of life" (John 8:12).

God is the light, the living light that shines darkness into nonexistence. Follow Him to a better place in your life.

Composure

There are days when my soul
Is in need of recharging
'Cause I drag about with purpose low
Moving away from the light that inspires,
Light that guides me on my path
To my purpose. To my destiny.

God understands that in my mortal self,
I will from time to time weaken,
That's when He manifests His will
Through things I hear or see,
To bring me back to the course He's set
With strength, wisdom, and love: all free.

Faith

Whatever is ailing you,
Look toward the sky,
Pray for answers divine
And usher in a new dawn.

Always There

Moon and sun
Constant companions are they,
Beginning and ending each day
Whether at rest or play,
Inside or out – moving about,
They're both on which we depend.

Moon and sun
Constant companions are they,
Taking back seats on cloudy days
To make room for the rain and snow
Only to resurface as they go,
Continuing to cast their magical glow.
The eyes of God watching over us,
All the time.

Part 6
A Godlike State of Mind

Just Stop It!

And the dreams continue. Last night, I was singing with the rest of the congregation during a Sunday morning church service. Suddenly, a jazz piece started to play, the people started to dance enthusiastically, and so did I. Looking over my shoulder, I told the person behind me, "Lord, we're dancing in the church." This behavior continued until we realize that what we were doing was not right. Then we stopped dancing and started sending our praises to God through song.

The next morning, I rehashed the dream over and over until I reached the following conclusion: When we find out that we're not in tune with God's teachings, we should stop and do the right thing. We will all go astray during various times in our lives, but the lesson is in learning from our errors.

Are you learning from your errors?

What Would Jesus Say?

Sunday night, my husband and I were watching television when a commercial with what I call inappropriate content graced the television screen. I'm sure you can think of many such scenes. My husband asked me, "What would Jesus say?" I thought about it for a minute and said, "Jesus would probably ask them, 'Did you read my book?'" Well, I don't know what Jesus would say, but if the people were constant readers of His word, maybe they would have written a commercial with appropriate content.

You Never Know Unless You Try

Success is knowing the odds but acting anyhow.

Today, I received my Professional Teaching License. It was a big deal for me, because this journey started way back in 1989. After moving to

Wisconsin from Nebraska, I was blessed to get a teaching position in the public school system. However, I worked under a provisional license and needed to take some additional courses before the Department of Public Instruction would issue a Professional Teaching License. I was disappointed, because I had in my possession teaching licenses from Nebraska and South Carolina.

I taught one year and did not return the next, because my husband and I decided that I would stay home and take care of our newly born twins. As our children grew, I would use my training as a teacher to prepare them for success in school. While my children were in second grade, I enrolled, in 1998, at the University of Wisconsin at Milwaukee to take the first of two courses that would move me closer to obtaining my Professional Teaching License.

Years later, during the month of September 2009, I decided to restart the process of obtaining my teaching credentials: I filled out the application, sent forms to the colleges where I received my education, sent forms to employers for verification of work experience, and walked over to the police station with the rest of the application, where I was fingerprinted, in order to complete the application process.

A couple of weeks later, the Wisconsin Department of Public Instruction sent me a letter outlining the courses that I needed to take before the department would issue a teaching license. I enrolled again at the University of Wisconsin at Milwaukee to take the last course, with the intention of starting classes in January 2010.

Urged by an inner voice from God, I had my transcripts sent to the Department of Public Instruction to show my completion of the course that I took in 1998. Additionally, I filled out the employer verification form, which I didn't fill out initially because I didn't think that the department would accept the teaching experience and work experience from the school that I opened in 1998. Despite my reservation, I sent the information.

Two weeks later, I removed a large white envelope from my mailbox. I opened the envelope expecting to see more information about further requirements for obtaining a teaching license, but careful observation past the first page revealed what I was working toward—my teaching license from the state of Wisconsin! This experience has taught me that from good deeds come good deeds, and you never know what the outcome will be unless you try.

Regardless of the end results to any situation, all is done under God's will and plan for our lives. He has the perfect solution to our problems. Infinite is He.

Infinite is He

God is an endless body of water
that never ebbs or runs dry,
No borders or shores in sight
With everything that we'll ever need
Accessible through a simple request: prayer.

Bliss

You are truly a work of art,
Made in the image of God,
Filled with immeasurable gifts
By a Father to his child.

Still in Control

Look for a road that leads somewhere and for that location, rely on God

Sometimes our concerns show up in our dreams—some giving solutions, some giving another view of the problem, and still others leaving you more puzzled. In this dream, I find myself at the wheel of an out-of-control wood-paneled station wagon. I could not stop the car because the brakes did not work. There was nothing I could do.

This was a frightening dream. As the car sped down the street, I looked in the rearview mirror and could see in the luggage area the top portion of a head bobbing up and down, and in the seat behind me, demons laughing and yelling in excitement, while we continued to speed down the street.

I remember praying and asking God for help. I kept yelling at the demons, "I don't know how or when, but the Lord is going to intervene!" Ahead I saw a gas station. As the car got closer to it, I kept thinking how nice it would be if I could pull into the station and bring the car to a complete stop. The car continued to barrel toward the station, and the noise within the car got louder. Without any indication, the car came to a complete stop without causing any damage to me or the car.

When I woke up, the words "I don't know how, when, or where, but the Lord is going to intervene" were imprinted on my mind. The Lord was in control all the time, even though it appeared otherwise. He is in control of our lives and will give us a safe and peaceful place to land, if we believe.

We can put our hands down because there are some things that we cannot control. God's hands are mightier than ours.

Hands Down

I can put my hands down,
I'm not holding up the world,
Free to make mistakes and be
whatever is natural and just.
The world is in good hands,
It's been there since the beginning of time.

I can move about my day
knowing that I too am in good hands,
Free to explore, try, succeed or fail.
At the end of the day, I am safe,
resting in God's infinite haven.

November 21st

Himalaya

After turning the television to another morning show, *Today*, I decide to go upstairs to get a box of incense. From the drawer of my nightstand, I pull out the box of incense called "Himalaya." While visiting Cornell University in Ithaca, New York, on a college tour with my two children and husband, I bought this box, along with a different box of incense.

As Hoda and Kathie Lee hosted the last hour of *Today*, they came to a segment of the show where they introduced a mystery guest. When they maneuvered their way into the room where the guest awaited, there stood a yoga instructor with the name Himalaya.

The word Himalaya creates a picturesque scene of gigantic mountains with snow-capped peaks, the freshest of air, a place where one can renew the soul. With all of their beauty, nothing can compare to the beauty, the peace, the comfort, the love, and the promise of eternal life that we have in God.

God is the Master Creator whose creations keep giving throughout time.

Part 7
The Spirit of Christmas

Anticipation

I'd plan to get a tree
And decorate it from tip to trunk
So when my children came home
It would be there for them to see.
But when I told them of my plans,
They responded, "wait on me,"
Until then an empty space remains
Igniting all kinds of feelings within
For the times that lie ahead
As we sit and talk throughout the night,
Oh! Oh! What a beautiful sight.

The Selfishness in Humanity

Some of us arrive earlier and some of us get to where we are going later—that's life.

Many of the problems that affect humanity today are the result of some people who lack the self-discipline to effectively plan for things. Instead, they want to have things when they want them and how they want them. This selfish behavior can have evil connotations if it hurts someone else, and it becomes a crime on humanity when this behavior affects a massive group of people. I believe this behavior to be self-destructive and in the long run, you lose more than you gain.

I remember my husband and me going out to buy some Halloween candy—anticipating the arrival of Halloween in a couple of days. On that day, I decided to drive instead of my husband, because he does most of the driving when we go places together. As we're driving down the road, I come to a complete stop at the traffic light, because it turned red. There are now other cars behind me. While we wait, a couple crosses the busy street. They get to the median and continue walking across the street to get to the other side. The traffic light turns green, and I ease out to make the left turn but have to wait until the couple clears the path. All of a sudden, the driver behind me blows his car horn. I'm thinking at that time, "What in the world?"

Could this person not see the couple crossing the street in front of me? Was he in that big of a hurry? What was I supposed to do—run over the couple? Some people are in too much of a hurry. Wherever he was headed, it was not as important as making sure that these people safely crossed the road.

As the couple reached the other side of the street, I made my turn and continued on my way. The black car with dark tinted windows eventually disappeared out of sight. I think some people who drive these types of cars hide behind the dark windows and use them as an extra incentive to be rude and careless—at least it appears to be true in this case. People who are without a sense of humanity while driving are the ones who are prone to causing accidents.

There is nothing more important in the world than displaying Christ-like behavior wherever we go. Let us be the best caretakers of each other.

Christmases of Old

Stay in Christ and live that life.

I continue to write poems throughout the Thanksgiving and Christmas holidays. While writing and listening to Christmas carols on the radio, I can still feel the excitement that I felt when I was a little girl over having a decorated Christmas tree in the house. This year a decorated Scotch pine tree stands in front of the living room window. Its scent moves throughout the house. I wish that more people would carry the beauty of the Christmas tree in their hearts and minds and use those warm feelings to guide their behavior, not only at Christmas but throughout the years to come.

Imagine having the spirit of Christmas stirring within our hearts and using it to communicate with people in our communities, then the country, and then the world. Imagine!

Christmas Tree

Away to the tree farm we went
In search of a special one
That will stand majestically in place
Throughout the long awaited holidays.

Plenty of firs and scotch pines
Covered from head to toe
With a blanket of freshly fallen snow,
Awaits each to be carried home.

Trekking in snow just below the knee
To inspect the trees as we walk about,
The shape, the branches, the color, the height,
Until at a distance, there it stood.

Everything we were expecting
And more so as we shook the branches
To remove the snow and better reveal
What we saw from a distance.

Gently removed from its sturdy base,
Carried by one in front and back,
Tied firmly to the roof of our car,
A smooth ride to where we had begun.

Now, it stands in its special place,
Sparkling lights of red, white, green, yellow and blue
With dangling earrings in the same colors too,
Topped with our familiar star from years passed,
A symbol of faith, love and joy.

A Brown Paper Bag

We reach for things that are far away, paying no attention to those at hand, only to find at a later time that what we needed was right there within reach.

Snow is everywhere. There is snow at the back, front, sides, and even large drifts of snow are hanging from the trees. I can see its glitter as the sun reflects its rays upon it. Mesmerized by the whiteness and brightness of the snow outside, my soul is warmed by childhood memories of Christmases when I would get a lunch-sized brown bag filled with oranges, apples, pecans, and Christmas candy. A bulging bag placed next to my gifts under the Christmas tree on Christmas morning.

Did you get a brown paper bag filled with goodies? Do you give brown bags to others? It's never too late to start a tradition.

Glitter

As the sun cast its shadow
Upon the fluffy snow below,
Magically appears flickers of color
In red, green blue and yellow.

Red bows at the corner of each post
A view of the deck out back,
A much needed break in a sea of white,
Marveling at a spectacular sight.

The Biggest Gift Ever

God sends us gifts throughout the year: look for them.

Weeks from now, Christians will celebrate the birth of our Lord and Savior, Jesus Christ. Christmas songs are coming from the radio, and I look forward to the arrival of my children from college. My soul rejoices! And although Christmas comes during the last month of the year, it marks the beginning, to me, of a new year. After all, God is the Alpha and the Omega.

As I have grown and continue to mature in God's teachings, I know that we can be all that we need to be through His teachings. There is not enough room to hold all of the gifts God has for us, because He continues to give continuously. All we have to do is acknowledge Him in all that we do, believe, and we will receive. Let us give thanks to God throughout the years for giving us the most precious gift ever, and through His Son, Jesus, we have everlasting life.

Never Forget

All inhabits of the earth
Singing in your native tongue,
Let us all look toward the heavens
Giving praises and thanking Him
For what He has done.

All inhabitants of the earth,
Close your eyes and just imagine
That night and what it was like
On our dear Savior's birth.

All inhabitants of the earth
Reserve now in your hearts,
A place for His Majesty,

A beacon of light
That guides humanity through the night.

All inhabitants of the earth
With our eyes focused on the star,
Follow, never wavering
But always remembering
His love for each and every one.

Final Thoughts

Time alone—a soul reborn.

Regardless of where you are on your journey, or to what destination you are traveling, remember that God is with us always. And when obstacles appear on our roads, and when it seems that the challenges are too big, we have all we need in God. He surrounds us with His love and His angels, and guides us wherever we might travel. He must be our everything, because everything can be found in Him. God is the author of all.

Through prayer, we have access to God at all times. I encourage you to make silent time a priority. It is only during this time that you can hear what God is saying. Pay attention to the incidences that you might dismiss as coincidental. Record these happenings and come to your own conclusion. God is our biggest gift ever, and He continues to give all the time.

I pray that your purpose in life is revealed as you continue to offer your prayers to God. With God's divine guidance, our souls are renewed, and our lives become meaningful.

Blessings!

Thoughts and Knocks

Thoughts and Knocks

Thoughts and Knocks

Fun List Continued:

Back Cover

Revered Moments

While growing up in the countryside in South Carolina, Dr. Altamese (Pelzer) Moore always attended church with her grandmother on Sunday mornings. The pastor's sermons echoed with words like "God sees everything you do" and "God will always be with you."

As Dr. Moore continued her life's journey, the pastor's words were always close. Struggling with stints of unemployment, major personal decisions to be made, uncertainty, and confusion, Moore becomes an eyewitness to just how much God loves His children.

On two separate occasions during these difficult times, Moore encounters the appearance of an angelic being. It was during these moments that she knew God is always listening, watching, and would also be there to lead and guide us.

There are some occurrences that cannot be explained, because they did not originate from this world. God's power cannot be measured by human understanding. Moore, an educator, knows that God is always accessible through prayer and obedience.

This book features Dr. Moore's personal stories with divine intervention and inspirational poems that will renew your faith while helping you develop a closer relationship with God.

www.ingramcontent.com/pod-product-compliance
Lightning Source LLC
Chambersburg PA
CBHW071717040426
446CB00011B/2104